MAGRETS & MUSHROOMS

More recipes from South-West France

JEANNE STRANG
Author of Goose Fat & Garlic

ckbk

This edition first published in Great Britain in 2024 by ckbk

An imprint of 1000 Cookbooks Ltd

www.ckbk.com

Hardcover ISBN 978 1 73847 063 1
Paperback ISBN 978 1 73847 064 8
Electronic ISBN 978 1 73847 060 0

A Cataloguing in Publication record for this title is available from the British Library.

Typeset by Chrysalis DSS
Cover design by Dale Walker

Cover illustration by Tony Gregson

CONTENTS

FOREWORD

In 1961, long before it was fashionable, Paul and Jeanne Strang bought an abandoned farmhouse in the Aveyron, in the heart of South-West France - La France Profonde. He was a solicitor, she a book editor, and thus began a 60 year love affair with the Aveyron, their neighbours and the French way of life.

In the crowded field of cookery books, few achieve the status of classics. The works of Elizabeth David and Jane Grigson, and mega-sellers such as Robert Carrier's *Great Dishes of the World* (1963) and *Delia's Complete Cookery Course* (1992), are exceptions, remaining perpetually in print and on literally millions of British bookshelves.

For the cookbook connoisseur, Jeanne Strang rides equally high. *Goose Fat & Garlic* (1991) is a work of supreme culinary scholarship, reprinted and revised over thirty years, more than 70,000 copies sold, still readily available. We learn about the region and its history, its geography and farming practices, but above all we learn about its people and their traditions. There doesn't exist a more authentic, personal and fastidiously researched introduction to the life and mores of rural France.

Jeanne's publisher, Kyle Cathie, knew she had something exceptional on her hands from the outset. Peter Mayle wrote, 'Pangs of hunger forced me to stop half way through the cassoulet recipe… fascinating and delicious, it almost tempts me to leave Provence'. Patricia Wells commented, 'Rich with anecdotes, legends, the stuff of real daily life in South-West France, this is the kind of book you'll carry right into the kitchen, focusing your energies on meaty daubes, hearty country soups, simple salads dressed with rich, local walnut oil. As you turn the pages you can almost smell the potatoes cooking away with the garlic and parsley, and hear the sizzle of the fire as the leg of lamb turns on the spit. Culling recipes from the baker's wife, the cafe owner, anyone who would listen, Jeanne Strang has produced a book with a ring of authenticity; a must for all cooks with a sense of curiosity and a dose of ambition.'

For author and France expert Carolyn Boyd, 'it gives a wonderful insight into a way of life in which nothing is wasted and everything is tasty. It's a wonderful testament to the region and its people.' For chef Tom Conran, 'It's one of my favourite cookbooks. Untainted by modernity, the recipes read like folk stories of a great culinary tradition which has been passed down through generations for centuries, but which — like a rare animal or plant— is now in danger of extinction.'

Reading this book in 2000 persuaded me to take a walking holiday in the region, and resulted in my moving there in 2004: one of many lives changed by it. Alison Stattersfield, a French cookery enthusiast with a house in the Lot, fell so deeply love with the recipes that she decided to cook her way through them all (there are more than 200) as a retirement project.

When Jeanne died in August 2023, she left a complete manuscript for a new book, *Magrets & Mushrooms*. As well as a further 138 recipes—now accompanied in the digital edition by Alison Stattersfield's photographs—this book is a recognition that times change, even in the South West of France. 'Families that had depended on having a motor car, and probably an old and dilapidated one at that, suddenly found everyone had a car of their own… Neighbours of ours who had never travelled as far as their own county town saw their offspring beginning to enjoy the pleasures of holidays away from home.'

Many of the recipes are traditional, discovered by Jeanne since her first book was published. Others nod in the direction of modernity— though never 'cheffiness'— and make use of ingredients unheard of in the earlier era: flat peaches, butternut squash, raz-el-hanout and filo pastry. Stick blenders, liquidizers and processors now take their place alongside earthenware pots and cast iron *poêles*.

The book includes several recipes involving foie gras, a subject on which Jeanne wrote in depth. For a characteristically considered and compassionate study of that issue, I would refer you to the essay she wrote for *Gastronomica* in 2007. For those seeking wines to accompany the recipes, the definitive guide remains *South-West France: The Wines and Winemakers* (2009) written by her husband Paul and lavishly photographed by Jason Shenai (her niece's husband).

What continues to shine bright in *Magrets & Mushrooms* is Jeanne's deep affection for the region: a unique blend of warmth and wisdom, leavened with wry observation and gentle humour. If one thinks of *Goose Fat* as a love letter to South-West France, this book is a renewal of vows, and deserves a place in the bookshelf of every Francophile and admirer of authentic French country cooking.

ORLANDO MURRIN
President, Guild of Food Writers

MAGRETS & MUSHROOMS

A MAGRET DE CANARD IS the breast of a duck that has undergone the ecstasies and pains of being force-fed with corn-maize so as to produce foie-gras. Magret derives from the word maigre, meaning the lean meat of the bird.

Ever since the famous chef André Daguin from Auch introduced the *magret* to the world in 1976 (he says he recovered it from memories of his childhood and was not the inventor), it has become a mainstay of the South-West repertoire. Chefs have invented many variations on the cooking and presentation of a *magret*, sometimes with honey, otherwise with a *compôte* of apples, even with a range of oriental spices. We have enjoyed it with a short sauce made from plum brandy and verjuice, but to us nothing beats André's simple method, and we add some words of advice of our own.

MAGRET DE CANARD

Fattened Duck Breast

1. Score the fat side crosswise several times with a sharp knife, cutting the fat down to but not through the flesh below.
2. Be generous with the seasoning, especially coarse salt, which should be rubbed carefully into the fat.
3. We like to give the *magret* a preliminary marinade for a couple of hours with bay leaves, thyme, seasonings (including a little *piment d'Espelette)* and a couple of tablespoons of Armagnac.
4. Be sure to allow as much of the fat to run before cooking the *magret*. It will yield a surprisingly large amount of beautiful duck fat, which you can use to cook any accompanying potatoes–*pommes de terre rissolées* for example (page 112), which go wonderfully well with a *magret*.

5. For this preliminary process, place the *magret* fat-side down on a griddle or in a stout frying pan, which should be warmed to as low a heat as possible. As the fat runs, drain it into a bowl. The fat side of the *magret* will gradually become golden and the joint will start to shrink and to curl.
6. Raise the heat to further crisp and colour the fat side of the joint and turn it over for a minute or two before extinguishing the heat altogether. Allow to rest for a quarter of an hour or so before serving. Carve it in thin slices which should be a uniform pink all the way through.

We first came upon the *magret* when staying at the Hotel Ripa Alta in Plaisance in Gascony. Monsieur Coscuella, the owner-chef, grilled them like steaks and served them pink with a sauce made from the pan juices with added green peppercorns.

Lou Magret au Poivre Vert

Duck Breasts with Green Peppercorns

2 magrets de canard
12 green peppercorns, chopped

Remove the peppercorns from their brine if you have bought them preserved. Cook the *magrets* as above, and when you turn up the heat towards the end, add the peppercorns. Remove the *magrets* to a warm serving dish and allow the peppercorns to simmer for a few minutes in the pan juices.

Although the goose, increasingly seldom to be found, is undoubtedly the monarch of the farmyard (*la basse-cour)*, its place is gradually being usurped by the duck, which is easier to rear, needing only two feeds a day instead of the three prescribed for the goose when it is prepared for the ultimate sacrifice. Whole ducks are not very often seen even at market, because the bird so easily joints itself into manageable pieces with which to make *confit*, abundantly sold *sous-vide*, enabling the consumer to keep the packets for weeks at a time and, coming from a reputable source, can be nearly as good as *confit* made at home.

Other duck recipes appear in the chapter headed *La Basse-Cour* *(page 42)*.

MUSHROOMS GALORE

If you go out into the woods or fields mushroom hunting without success, here are four good reasons why you may have failed to find any.

One, a very hot, dry summer may not have been followed by the right amount of rain in conjunction with more warmth.

Two, if you hoped to find *cèpes* you did not go out looking five days after a downpour on a waning moon.

Three, you did not get up early enough. Have you ever wondered why on some mornings there are strange cars parked at the side of wooded country lanes, sometimes bearing a numberplate of a neighbouring *département*? They often belong to *braconniers*, mushroom poachers, who make quite a picking out of selling the fungi on at their local markets or elsewhere.

The fourth reason is that you may not have been looking in the right spot. Any locals (even your best friends) whom you ask for directions, will either not answer, or will misdirect you. It is all part of the great mushroom hunting omerta which many French country men are passionate about.

You can tell the freshness of a *cèpe* by the underside of the cap. Unlike other fungi, it is made up not of gills but a sponge-like mass of tubes. When fresh the underside is cream-coloured but this changes to an acid green with age. Smaller, firm specimens are better and tastier to cook with than big ones. Their strong flavour is unlike any other fungus, and one or two *sautéed* with potatoes will flavour the whole dish quite wonderfully. To cook a dish of *cèpes,* clean them, slice the caps and cut their bulbous stems into rounds. Sear them in hot oil, then reduce the heat, cover the pan and simmer for 10-15 minutes, adding seasonings, chopped garlic and parsley halfway through. If cooking them *à la Gasconne* the stalks should be chopped and cooked separately with diced *jambon de campagne,* this mixture then thickened with a little flour and some white wine to make a sauce in which the caps, previously fried, are finished. Cèpes freeze well or can be bottled or dried. Packets of dried ones are a good buy as they reconstitute well after a soaking in water for an hour or so. A few will transform any sauce or casserole. Use approximately one fifth of the weight you would use of fresh mushrooms. They have a particular affinity with rabbit or game of any kind and of course, make a fabulous omelette.

Many British and even French, people are nervous of mushrooming as they have heard lurid accounts of serious illness, even death, resulting from eating poisonous varieties. If you are in any doubt, you can take your specimens to the pharmacy for identification. And you can rest assured that if you buy mushrooms at market, they are known edible varieties– *cèpes, morilles, girolles, chanterelles, mousserons* or *coulemelles.*

Morilles are rather rare and highly prized, growing in spring in open woodland or by roadsides, under ash, elm or apple trees. In appearance they are quite different, their heads looking like pixie hats made of brown sponge. Their stalks have no flavour, so are best removed. Sand collects in the honeycomb-like caps, so they need careful cleaning. The best way is to dip the heads in salt water or white wine and agitate them in it to remove any grit. They should be well cooked (they are poisonous when raw) and are best *à la crème,* or as they are served in the Béarn, *sautéed* with *jambon de Bayonne* and served with a glass of Jurançon.

Girolles, also known as *chanterelles,* are the apricot-coloured, trumpet-shaped fungi that appear in late spring and wet summers and are perhaps the next-most prized after *cèpes.* They have a delicate but peppery flavour and go well with eggs. When really fresh they contain a lot of moisture which must be eliminated first by a quick *sauté* in oil. Discard any juices and, in a clean pan, continue their cooking. Cream, garlic and parsley are the best seasonings. *Trompettes de la mort* you may sometimes find at market. They are similar in shape to *girolles* and are interchangeable in recipes.

Mousserons, known in Britain as fairy-ring mushrooms, have a small. rounded cap and a very thin stalk, which is hard and should be discarded. Our local market had a stall selling good quantities of them, so I was prompted to consider making *La Recoulette* which is a delicious quiche originating in the Auvergne. (You can find the recipe in *Goose Fat & Garlic*). As I waited my turn at the stall a *gendarme* approached and engaged the stall holder for some time in what I took to be official business. I then discovered he was queue-jumping and really wanted to buy a large quantity of the *mousserons.* I must have looked surprised as he then leaned over and told me how to cook them _ "wonderful with a pork chop or a *sauté de veau à la crème".* I have collected many recipes at markets over the years but never before one from a *gendarme.*

At the very end of the season, and then only in some years, you may be lucky to find the spectacular *oronge*, rated by some as the finest of all mushrooms in the South-West. Its official name is *Amanita caesarea*, because of the predilection of Roman Emperors for the species. But beware; there is also a near-related variety that is toxic, distinguishable by a much redder cap. If in doubt, take advice before contemplating cooking this spectacular mushroom.

INTRODUCTION

SINCE MY *GOOSE FAT & Garlic* (Kyle Books, 1991) was written thirty years ago, cooking in South-West France has expanded its frontiers as well as keeping its original features.

During the last half of the 20th century, the rapid growth of the French economy gradually brought benefits to the country districts of the South-West. Work away from the land became available to the many young people who had been the fruit of the government-sponsored baby boom of the 1950s.

Cheap loans encouraged young couples to move from old and often primitive family homes and to build themselves a new house. Older families, to escape the rigours and discomforts of their old but beautiful homesteads, moved into new homes, often built in their own farmyards. Sadly, many of the old houses were allowed to crumble into irreparable ruin. Modern kitchens began to replace the primitive cooking arrangements of the old farmhouse, modern cookers became a status symbol, accessories such as electric kettles, blenders and even the microwave became commonplace.

Families that had depended on having a motor car, and probably an old and dilapidated one at that, suddenly found everyone had a car of their own, nowadays regarded as indispensable for country living. Neighbours of ours who had never travelled as far as their own county town saw their offspring beginning to enjoy the pleasures of holidays away from home. Children of today cannot believe what they are told by their grandparents about the rigours of life as it was in their day, not so long ago.

And yet a deep affection for the past persists. The many Auvergnats and Aveyronnais who moved to Paris to escape poverty at home created many of the bistrots and cafés that today provide the metropolis with a variety of food traditional to the

South-West. Fifty years ago, *cassoulet* was barely mentioned in the tourist guides to Paris restaurants, but today no fewer than 23 list it as a speciality, more than any other French dish. Young town-dwellers flock to their family roots in the country for their holidays and festive occasions in the hope that their elders have not forgotten how to prepare the dishes they loved in their childhood. *Saucisses aligot* remains the favourite offering at country *fêtes*, and in what other part of France do they still prepare such delicious *foie gras* and *confits* for visitors to take home to their modern in the cities?

Alongside the modern taste for exotic foods imported from anywhere in the world, the care for tradition remains, a tradition that proves its value through family ties and a love of the *pays* from which it springs.

It may be useful to preface this book with a few general hints and observations.

1. All recipes are given for 4 people unless otherwise stated.
2. Quantities are given in metric measurements.
3. Butter refers to unsalted butter unless otherwise indicated.
4. You will need an assortment of heavy ovenproof casseroles with tight-fitting lids, preferably with cast-iron bottoms.
5. Oven temperatures are given in Centigrade, Fahrenheit and gas mark numbers.

LES SOUPES

DESPITE THE PASSAGE OF TIME, soup remains the first course for many a South-West evening meal, sometimes the entire meal. Soup is an incomparable preparation for the digestion, a preparation for what, if anything, is to follow. There are recipes for all seasons of the year, many of which have changed in character and weight with the arrival of modern kitchen gadgetry such as the liquidizer. The ease with which a purée can now be made has resulted in a taste for a thicker style of soup, though for many, especially in the summer months, unthickened stock remains the preferred base. For others, a good soup is an ideal way of profiting from the surplus of vegetables from the *potager*.

Devoted cooks will continue to prepare basic stocks from the carcasses and leftovers of the family chicken. Some will set aside for the purpose the bones of veal, beef or the family pig. The commercial stock cubes now universally available should not be spurned but they offer no comparison to a freshly prepared stock. Nor should the unconsumed juices of a home-cooked braise of pork or veal be overlooked as a flavour-boost to the simplest of soups.

Soups are usually consumed warm rather than hot; indeed, the British insistence that everything should be consumed so hot that you have to wait for it to cool, or on plates or dishes that are too hot to touch, seems to our French neighbours a strange way of approaching food.

Soups will reflect the changing seasons and the availability of ingredients. There will be some for whom the Lenten fast is still obligatory, at least on Good Friday itself when this traditional stomach-warmer will finally finish the lean times and prepare for the ubiquitous burst of Easter *gourmandise* to follow.

La Soupe de Vendredi Saint

Good Friday soup

400 g chickpeas, soaked for 24hours
1 litre water
60 g duck or goose fat
1 large onion, chopped
2 cloves garlic, chopped
salt and pepper
2 slices white country bread, cut into cubes, to serve

Rinse and drain the chickpeas, then cook them in salted water for 2 hours, or until tender. Heat half the fat in a frying pan and cook the onion and garlic until soft and just starting to colour. Add to the chickpeas and liquidize in a blender or food processor. Reheat gently and season to taste.

Heat the remaining fat in a frying pan, add the bread cubes and fry until brown and crisp. Serve the croutons with the soup.

Another one-course meal can be made from this traditional, rustic cheese soup. Even a salad to follow might seem superfluous. During the past 30 years many of the mountain cheesemakers in the Cantal and Aveyron have abandoned their *burons* where they traditionally made their own cheese and butter. That way of life has turned out to be too lonely as well as too hard. The herdsmen now more frequently market their produce through local cooperatives, such as at Laguiole. A handful of *burons* still exist but many have become tourist attractions for curious food-lovers anxious to explore the delights of home-made *aligot*.

A string of local, controlled *appellations* has sprung up, the best requiring the exclusive use of unpasteurized milk from which cheeses such as Cantal, Salers and Laguiole are made and marketed all over the South-West. Cheese soup has always been a favourite in this part of France, so it is not surprising that one of these wonderful cheeses finds its way into this simple but delicious interpretation.

La Soupe au Fromage

Cheese soup

2 tbsp duck or goose fat (sunflower oil at a pinch)
2 onions, sliced
2 leeks, finely sliced
slices of country bread (NOT steam-baked), cut 1cm thick
200 g Salers, Laguiole or Cantal cheese
1.25 litres chicken stock
salt and pepper

Preheat the oven to 180C/350F/gas mark 4.

Heat the fat in a frying pan and add the onions and leeks. Cook slowly until soft but not coloured.

Line the base of a large earthenware dish with a layer of the bread. Cover with one third of the cheese and half the leek and onions. Repeat the process and finish with another layer of bread, then the remaining cheese. Add enough stock to cover, season and cook uncovered in the oven for 1 hour until the stock is almost absorbed. For a thinner consistency, add more hot stock before serving.

There are many recipes for garlic soup but the one that follows is not only the most tasty of all but is brought to perfection by the use of the pink garlic that is the speciality of the Lautrec region in the Tarn, just south of Albi. Each year during the first week of

August, Lautrec holds its annual garlic *fête*, which attracts thousands of visitors. You can buy heads of the bulb itself, as well as all manner of elaborate artefacts and decorative objects made from garlic. At lunchtime, visitors collect in the village hall to enjoy this speciality.

La Soupe à l'Ail Rose de Lautrec

Pink Lautrec garlic soup

1 litre stock or water
4-8 pink garlic cloves, preferably from Lautrec, chopped
55 g vermicelli
2 tsp mustard
2 large or 4 small eggs, separated
200 ml sunflower oil
salt and pepper

Bring the stock or water to a boil in a large pan, then throw in the chopped garlic and the vermicelli. Simmer until the pasta is cooked (7-10 minutes).

Meanwhile, beat together the mustard, egg yolks, salt and pepper, then gradually beat in the sunflower oil until the mixture thickens like a mayonnaise.

Allow the garlic broth to cool a little, or add a little cold water to hasten the process, then vigorously whisk in the egg whites. Dilute the 'mayonnaise' mixture with a ladleful of the broth, then gently pour it into the soup and stir well. Check the seasoning. If the soup has cooled too much, reheat it very gently.

Serve with slices of fresh country bread.

o

Just as in times gone by when many of the principal French grape varieties were brought to France from distant lands by pilgrims, so nowadays holidaymakers returning from trips to Spain or Morocco have introduced a greater use of spices into their home-cooking, a trend augmented by the rise in immigration over the past 50 years. Gazpacho was at one time regarded as a philistine import, but today it is to be found everywhere, although not in this version of the recipe, which was entrusted to us by Madame Albespy who features it at her remote country *auberge* in the upper Lot Valley. One wonders where she got it from; perhaps from her goat-rearing neighbours near Entraygues on the vertiginous slopes of the Lot?

La Granita de Gazpacho à la Crême de Cabécou

Tomato and goats' cheese ice

400 ml fresh tomato juice
1 tsp harissa paste
1 tbsp wine vinegar
60 g caster sugar
1 tbsp tomato concentrate dissolved in 100 ml water
200 g fresh goats' cheese
4 tbsp yogurt
pepper
basil leaves, shredded or chopped

Stir the harissa paste into the tomato juice and mix well. Add the vinegar, sugar and dissolved tomato concentrate. Freeze, stirring the mixture every so often.

Serve in large goblets. Top with the cheese softened with the yogurt and lightly seasoned with pepper. Decorate with the basil leaves.

o

Here is another gazpacho recipe, believed to have been brought back to France from holidaymakers in Malaga. Although hardly typical of the South-West, it is an example of the kind of food that younger people in particular are looking for outside their family environment.

Le Gazpacho des Amandes Aux Raisins

Almond and grape cold soup

- 6 slices stale bread, crusts removed
- 130g almonds, blanched and skinned (or vacuum-packed)
- 3 cloves garlic, peeled
- 125 ml best olive oil
- 5 tbsp white wine vinegar
- 2 tsp salt
- 12 Muscat grapes, halved and seeded

Soak the bread in water for about 15 minutes until softened.

Combine the almonds and garlic in a food processor and pulse until the almonds are finely ground. Squeeze the water from the bread and add it to the food processor then blend to a smooth paste. With the motor still running, add the oil in a slow stream, followed by the vinegar and salt. Beat in 250 ml cold water.

Pour the mixture into a serving bowl, adding more water to taste. Taste for seasoning, add the grapes and serve.

o

As summer draws to an end, the *potagers* all over the countryside become overtaken by members of the squash family, their tentacle-like runners threatening to strangle the last few *haricots verts* trying to survive their onslaught. The delicate young courgettes make a delicious soup.

Le Potage Aux Courgettes

Courgette soup

butter and oil (sunflower)
3 medium-sized onions, chopped
1 kg courgettes, cut into small cubes
1 litre water
2 chicken stock cubes
crème fraîche
salt, pepper and grated nutmeg
walnut oil (optional), to serve

Heat enough butter and 1 tbsp oil in a large casserole (with a lid). Sweat the onions gently, covered, until they are translucent and soft. Add the courgettes and let them soften slightly, helped by a little salt, adding a bit more butter/oil if necessary.

Heat the water and dissolve the chicken stock cubes in it. Pour onto the onion and courgette mixture, bring to a simmer and cook, covered, for 15-20 minutes. Using a stick blender, carefully whizz the soup until creamy (although a few remaining chunks give it a bit of texture). Add *crème fraîche* and the seasonings to taste and reheat, but do not allow it to boil again. In walnut country, they drizzle a little walnut oil into each serving.

After the delicate young courgettes, which can mature alarmingly overnight into tough old marrows, come a wide range of pumpkins, ranging from the round orange *citrouille* to the flatter, bright red *potiron*. Many regard these as interchangeable in the kitchen although the *potiron* is said to have the sweeter flavour. Butternut squashes are now also fashionable. They roast beautifully to accompany red meats as well as making a delicious soup.

This recipe was given to us by a German friend, Elke, who lives part-time in the region, who no doubt she got it from some locals. The spices are our addition, to add a little warmth to the cooler autumn evenings.

La Soupe de Potiron Elke

Elke's pumpkin soup

- 1 tbsp duck fat
- 1 small/medium onion (all coarsely chopped)
- 2 cloves garlic (all coarsely chopped)
- the white part of one small leek (all coarsely chopped)
- 2 medium-sized carrots (all coarsely chopped)
- 500 g floury potatoes (all coarsely chopped)
- 500 g pumpkin flesh (all coarsely chopped)
- 500 ml chicken stock (or one stock cube dissolved)
- 1 tsp curry powder
- 1 tsp raz-el-hanout
- 2 tbsp whipping cream
- salt and pepper
- a handful of coriander leaves, finely chopped, to serve

Heat the fat in a large saucepan (with a lid), add the onion and garlic and soften in the fat without browning them. Add the leek and carrots and cook a little more. Add the stock, potatoes and pumpkin, season and cover. Cook gently for 40 minutes.

Allow to cool, then liquidize, adding the cream and spices. To serve, add the coriander leaves.

A more recent discovery in the South-West is the butternut squash, already familiar to British gardeners and cooks. One of our dear neighbours, Odile Mader, has given us the recipe for what she calls a *velouté*, a thickish purée. Her husband Alain confirms that this not a *soupe* in the old-fashioned sense, nor a *potage*; the style is familiar to those who buy ready-prepared soups in the shops, but none of those will taste as good as this.

Le Velouté de Butternut Mamie Odile

Mamie Odile's butternut squash soup

1 butternut squash
1 onion, chopped
1 chicken stock cube
2 tbsp crème fraîche
salt and pepper

Peel the butternut squash and cut it into cubes. Put the cubes in a large pan with the onion and chicken stock cube and cover with water. Bring to the boil and simmer for 20 minutes.

Mix a little of the liquid with the crème fraîche and return it to the pan, adding salt and pepper to taste. Cool, then liquidize in blender (or using a stick blender).

The South-West is land-locked apart from its Atlantic seaboard, where commercial fishing is dominated by the intrepid Basques operating largely out of St Jean de Luz and its neighbouring harbours. Fish soups are therefore unusual inland of that area but are nevertheless an important part of the Basque diet. The following recipe stipulates hake as a base, but in truth the locals will probably use whatever fish they find in their nets.

Le Ttoro

Basque fish soup

5 tbsp olive oil
2 onions, finely chopped
Head, skin and bones of hake or other white fish
2 cloves garlic, roughly chopped
bouquet garni
salt and 6 peppercorns
small piece of *piment d'Espelette* or ½ tsp ground *piment*
1½ litres water
600 g hake (or similar) cut into 4 cutlets
seasoned flour
4 langoustine tails (optional)
12-16 mussels (optional)
4 rounds French bread for croutons
1 tbsp chopped parsley

Heat 2 tbsp of the oil in a large casserole (with a lid) and gently cook the onions until golden. Add the fish head, skin and bones, garlic, bouquet garni, seasonings and water. Cover and simmer for 30 minutes. Strain the stock and return it to the casserole.

Dip the fish cutlets in the seasoned flour until evenly coated. Heat 2 tbsp of the oil in a frying pan and fry the cutlets for 1 minute on each side. Transfer to the hot stock (with the langoustines and mussels if using them) and simmer gently for 15 minutes.

In another frying pan, fry the bread rounds whole in the remaining oil until golden brown. Put a crouton in each of 4 serving bowls, sprinkle with the chopped parsley and garlic, then a fish cutlet on top and ladle over the fish stock. Add more *piment d'Espelette* if desired.

As the evenings draw in, thoughts turn to basic, heart-warming, old-fashioned soups such as this traditional one from our own district. Green vegetables no longer decorate the *potagers*, and Hallowe'en has disposed of most remaining pumpkins. Dried beans come into their own, together with the good old Aveyron stand-by: potatoes.

Le Potage Rouergat

The Rouergue soup

125 g dried white haricot beans
1½ tbsp goose fat
1 large onion, coarsely chopped
1 litre ham or chicken stock
450 g floury potatoes, peeled and chopped
salt and pepper
4 slices French bread, to serve

Put the beans in a pan with a tight-fitting lid, cover with cold water and leave to soak overnight.

Next day, bring the beans to the boil in the same water, boil hard for 10 minutes, then reduce the heat and cook gently, covered, for another 50 minutes. Drain and set aside.

Heat the fat in the same pan, add the onions and cook gently until soft. Add the stock and half of the potatoes. Bring to the boil, then cook over moderate heat for 30 minutes. Cool, then liquidize in blender (or using a stick blender).

Dice the remaining potatoes and add to the soup with the beans. Taste to test for seasoning, cover and simmer gently for another 30 minutes. To serve, put a slice of bread in the bottom of each serving bowl and pour the soup over. A meal in itself.

LES ENTRÉES

NOWADAYS, THE FIRST COURSE AT any meal, whether or not preceded by soup, can take many forms. Apart from the traditional *pâtés*, there are the many forms of *salade composée*, combining green leaves with anything that comes to hand. These seem to have superseded the old-fashioned *hors d'oeuvre* trolley on which one used to find simple dishes of cold lentils, marinated raw fish, grated carrots, celeriac *rémoulade*, as well as *charcuterie* and tomatoes.

A *salade composée* may well contain a selection of such ingredients, but will inevitably lie on a bed of lettuce, so that the need for a plain green salad to precede or follow the main dish of the meal is short-circuited. A potato salad will not be dressed with a true mayonnaise, which is now hardly ever available commercially because they are based on tasteless oils rather than olive oil. Then there is the regrettable balsamic vinegar, which is used as a satanically coloured decoration on ingredients that do not call for it. At home you can avoid its use, and we will always do so in reliance on our own vinegar-maker, while realizing at that, for some people, traditional vinegars are hard to come by, especially a good quality plain white wine vinegar, which seems to be unobtainable in supermarkets.

A simple recipe for asparagus manages to avoid these pitfalls.

Les Asperges au Fromage Frais de Chèvre et au Coriandre

Asparagus topped with goats' cheese and coriander

It is not always easy to find real tomatoes, as opposed to industrialized lookalikes, at a time when asparagus is in season. Just do your best with what is available.

The proliferation of goats' cheese has been one of the remarkable developments of the last 30 years. So many families have adopted a few of the animals, while others have made quite a successful and profitable sideline out of making cheeses from the milk of these loveable animals. They range from the fairly solid to the fresh and tangy. A sisterhood of nuns near us sell theirs at the local market and we call them the 'runny nunnies'. Delightful ladies and lovely produce.

5 asparagus spears per person
50 g fresh goats' cheese per person
fresh coriander, chopped
2 tomatoes, skinned, deseeded & sliced
1 onion, skinned, sliced into rings
lemony vinaigrette

Cook the asparagus until it is *al dente.* Mix the cheese with the chopped coriander. Arrange the asparagus on the plates and decorate with a spoonful of cheese, the tomato and onion. Trickle over the lemony, coriander-seasoned vinaigrette.

Other more original *entrées* betray ideas imported or borrowed from elsewhere in the south and even further afield as internationalism gradually overlays regional tradition. It is here that restaurant chefs in the South-West are often at their most inventive, introducing innovative flavours and blending them with the local traditional produce. Their *entrées* are often better than their main dishes. Any main course that follows the next dish, based on goats' cheese and filo pastry, would have to be very good indeed.

Les Croustillants de Chèvre

Goats' cheese in filo pastry

1 to 2 sheets filo pastry
4 discs of goats' cheese, each 5cm in diameter and 1cm thick
clarified butter
salad of bitter leaves
a handful of walnut pieces
walnut oil vinaigrette

Cut each pastry sheet into 8 rectangles, measuring 10 x 15 cm Allow enough pastry for each piece of cheese to make a good seal.

Using two thicknesses of pastry for each disc of cheese, place a disc at one end. Fold the pastry to make a parcel and seal the edges carefully, brushing with clarified butter, sealing well. Repeat with the other pieces of cheese.

Prepare four plates of bitter-leaf salad.

Fry the parcels in a minimum of clarified butter over medium heat for 2 minutes per side. Lay each on a bed of salad, sprinkle the walnut pieces and drizzle the dressing over. Serve immediately.

The *croustillants* should be golden, the outside crisp and the cheese melting within.

Courgette flowers, once considered the monopoly of the markets of Provence, have spread to the South-West. This is hardly surprising in a part of France where courgettes are so widely grown in everyone's *potager*.

Les Fleurs de Courgettes Farcies

Stuffed courgette flowers

For the filling
1 onion, finely chopped
2 courgettes, finely chopped
2 tbsp olive oil
1 clove garlic, chopped
2 tbsp chopped fresh herbs, such as parsley or marjoram
4 tbsp fresh breadcrumbs
salt and pepper
2 egg yolks

For the courgette flowers
1 bay leaf
8 courgette flowers
2-3 tbsp chicken stock
olive oil, for trickling

Prepare the filling by softening the onion and courgettes in 1 tbsp of oil over a medium heat for 2-3 minutes. Remove from the heat and stir in the garlic, herbs, breadcrumbs and seasoning. Allow to cool, then mix in the egg yolks.

Preheat the oven to 180C/350F/gas mark 4. Put the bay leaf in an oiled gratin dish. Carefully open each courgette flower and place a spoonful of the filling inside, tucking the tops in. Lay each on its side in the dish, add the chicken stock and trickle a little olive oil over each flower. Cover the dish with foil and bake for 15 minutes.

Les Beignets de Fleurs de Courgettes

Courgette flower fritters

For the fritter batter
3 tbsp olive oil
120 g plain flour, sifted
pinch of salt
150 ml lukewarm water
1 egg white
8-10 courgette flowers
vegetable oil for deep-frying

Prepare the fritter batter 2 hours ahead of time. Make a thickish cream by blending the oil into the sifted flour and salt, then beat in the water until smooth.

Just before frying, beat the egg white until stiff, then fold into the batter. Heat the oil to 190C/375F. Spike the flowers on a skewer or knife, dip them into the batter to coat well, then deep fry a few at a time for about 3 minutes until they are crisp and golden, turning them halfway through. Drain on kitchen paper and serve while they are hot and crisp. They need no accompaniment.

Far away from the sunshine of courgette flowers, the people of the upland hill country rejoice in a kind of fritter called *farsou* or *farsoun*. Basically featuring green vegetables and herbs, it may also contain pork or even leftovers from a *pot-au-feu*. Sometimes prunes replace the meat. There are as many different recipes as there are cooks, but the two following versions may be regarded as typical. Eat them hot: they are a bit solid when cold.

Lou Farsoun Rouergat

Fritter from the Rouergue

350 g fillet of pork
2 slices salt belly of pork
125 g flour
2 eggs
120 ml milk or water
salt, pepper

handful of chopped greens e.g. a mix of sorrel, spinach, chard, lettuce
1 tbsp chopped parsley
1 shallot, finely chopped
1 clove garlic, finely chopped
30 g *lard* (pork fat)

Mix together the meats. (You could use instead 500 g pure pork sausage meat.)

Make a thickish batter with the flour, beaten eggs and milk (or water). Season well. Stir in the mixed meat and the chopped greens. Add the shallot and garlic and mix all together.

Heat the lard in a thick-bottomed 24cm frying pan. Pour in the mixture, spreading it out to make a thick level pancake. Cook gently for 15-20 minutes, turn it over and cook for a further 10 minutes on the other side.

Lou Farsou

"To be made when the first dandelions appear and when the hens start to lay again". (Marie Rouanet in 'Appolonie' (Plon 1980)

150 g salt belly of pork, cut into small cubes
1 tbsp duck or goose fat
2 tbsp each parsley, chard, dandelion leaves and spinach, chopped
2 cloves garlic, chopped
2 cabbage leaves, chopped
150 ml milk
3 eggs
50 g flour
2 tbsp breadcrumbs
pepper and a little salt

Fry the pork in 1 tbsp of the fat until golden.

Combine the greens, garlic and cabbage with the milk and eggs, beat well– "with the energy of springtime", add the flour, breadcrumbs and seasonings, and mix together. Add the pork and its pan juices.

Heat the remaining 1 tbsp of fat in a 20cm frying pan, tip in the mixture and cook over a medium heat for about 4 minutes. It must cook through but not be allowed to burn. Loosen the pancake with a palette knife and slip it out on to a plate. Turn it over on to another plate, then slide it back into the frying pan and cook for a few minutes on the other side.

———o———

In the autumn, in addition to the giant pumpkins of various kinds, which can go a very long way indeed in a small household, the *potimarron* comes into its own. It is easily recognizable from its deep orange colour and modest dimensions. The name is derived from *potiron* (pumpkin) and *marron* (chestnut), because of its colour.

Being much smaller it can be made into a tasty *entrée*, or perhaps a main dish, depending on its size, for 2 people.

Le Potimarron Farci Aux Lardons

Pumpkin stuffed with bacon

Serves 2

1 potimarron
2 tbsp lardons
½ onion, chopped
2 tbsp grated Comtal cheese
salt and pepper

Heat the oven to 180C/350F/gas mark 4.

Cut the potimarron in half vertically and remove all the seeds. Gently fry the lardons and onion until the onion is softened and translucent. Fill each half *potimarron* with that mixture, put a tablespoonful of cheese on top of each and season well.

Place in an oiled roasting tin and cook for 40-45 mins until the flesh of the *potimarron* is soft.

Foie gras used to be regarded as the ultimate in gastronomic luxury, but its enjoyment today is within the reach of those with quite moderate incomes, and indispensable at times of celebration. Its comparative affordability is explained by the fact that the rearing of the birds is nowadays largely mechanized, with modern feeding methods cutting by 90% the traditional feeding time. Birds raised in this way no doubt satisfy the industrial *charcutiers*, but no restaurateur or *épicier* of quality would ever admit to dealing in industrialized *foie gras*, just as they would never admit to using anything but free-range poultry. But those who vaunt the merits of the traditional one-old-lady-to-one-bird approach are not just nodding in the direction of folklore. The knowing gourmet will insist that the quality of a good *foie gras* is pre-ordained almost from the bird's birth, and, as far as force-feeding is concerned, there is no substitute for the personal relationship that develops between the stuffer and the stuffed, calling for complicity, connivance and co-operation. The final days, even of a traditionally reared bird, may be uncomfortable or painful even, but for most of its life it has been spoilt, fed on the fat of the land and brought up almost as one of the family. Not so the intensively reared birds of the industrial farms.

In the old days *foie gras*, if it was to be preserved rather than used fresh, it was almost always put into sterilized jars or terrines. The more modern taste is for a *pâté* prepared several days ahead of time, but that will last a much shorter time afterwards than the old-fashioned terrine version. It can, however, be bought vacuum-packed in which the instructions on the pack will indicate its keeping capacity.

Le Foie Gras Entier Mi-Cuit

Whole foie gras half-cooked

Serves 6 to 8

2 fresh *foie gras* of duck (approx 900 g) or 1 of goose (approx 600 g)
2 tsp Armagnac
2 tsp vin doux naturel or port
2 tsp medium-sweet white wine
1 pinch each of grated nutmeg and cinnamon
salt and pepper

For the aspic jelly
150 ml strong chicken stock
1 tsp gelatine

Separate the lobes of the liver(s), then soak them in warm water for 1 hour.

Drain and pat the liver(s) dry with kitchen paper. Open pockets in each lobe with a small sharp knife, so that you can remove all the necessary veins. This is essential if the finished *pâté* is to cut easily and not tear.

Place the liver(s) in a shallow dish with the armagnac, wines, spices and seasonings. Turn to coat well, then leave to marinate overnight in the refrigerator.

Next day, allow the liver(s) to come to room temperature for 1 hour. Preheat the oven to 150C/300F/gas mark 2. Take a *terrine* that the livers will fit into when tightly packed, getting the top surface level to within 2cm of the top of the *terrine*. Pour the marinade over.

Prepare a *bain-marie* by filling a roasting tin to a depth of 2cm with water heated to 70C/160F. The temperature of the water and oven are important. Put your *terrine* into the roasting tin and cook uncovered for 35 minutes.

Remove the *terrine* from the oven and allow it to cool at room temperature, then refrigerate until required.

Well ahead of serving time, make the aspic jelly by warming the chicken stock. Add the gelatine, stir vigorously, then remove from the heat and pour into a shallow dish. Leave to cool, then chill.

To serve the *pâté,* unmould it on to a serving dish. Garnish with the aspic chopped into tiny pieces. Dip a knife into a jug of hot water before cutting each slice. Serve with fresh walnut bread or toast.

There are a number of other ways of enjoying *foie gras,* sometimes hot rather than cold.

Le Foie Gras Frais Aux Câpres

Whole foie gras cooked with capers

1 fresh *foie gras* of duck (about 450 g)
salt and pepper
2 tbsp brandy
1 tbsp duck or goose fat
60 g chopped shallot
1 tbsp flour
120 ml white wine
4 tbsp veal or chicken stock
60 g capers

Check that the liver is clean and free from gristle or blood vessels, soak it in milk for 1 hour, and dry on kitchen paper. Season and sprinkle with the brandy. Leave in the refrigerator for 2-3 hours.

Heat the fat in a casserole over a low to medium heat. Dry the liver again on kitchen paper and cook gently until it changes colour, turning it carefully. Remove from the casserole and put aside. Cook the shallot until softened, add the flour and stir until it starts to brown. Stir in the wine and stock and leave to simmer for 30 minutes over a very low heat.

Turn up the heat, put in the *foie gras,* then reduce the heat immediately. Simmer slowly for ten minutes. Rinse the capers (if they have been stored in vinegar) and add them at the end of the cooking time.

Slice the *foie gras*, arrange it on a serving plate and coat with the sauce. The *foie gras* should be so tender that it can, as is traditional, be eaten with a spoon.

Pasta was introduced into France in the 16th century by Catherine de Medici. In the South-West it has been a standby of the cuisine for a long time. It would be surprising if our local cooks had not found a way of marrying it with *foie gras*, although there are other ways too, in which it has been use locally.

Le Macaronade de Foie Gras

Macaroni with foie gras

100 g *cèpes* (20g if dried then reconstituted)
1 tbsp duck or goose fat
250 ml strong beef stock reheated (left over from oxtail, daube, etc)
salt, pepper
300 g dried macaroni or other pasta
1 tbsp sunflower oil
150 g fresh *foie gras* (goose or duck) or 100 g *foie gras mi-cuit*

Wipe the *cèpes* clean if using fresh ones. Otherwise rehydrate them and then wipe dry. Slice them into bite-sized pieces.

Melt the fat in a small pan, cook the *cèpes* very slowly without letting them go crisp, add the stock and season. Cover the pan and simmer slowly for 30 minutes.

Meanwhile, cook the pasta in boiling water with the oil. Strain and rinse in more boiling water.

Dice the *foie gras* and place it in the bottom of a deep, warmed bowl. Tip the hot pasta over and add the sauce. Mix well, check for seasoning and serve immediately.

Pasta turns up in various guises all over the South-West. In the Basque country, you will find various varieties (tagliatelle, spaghetti, macaroni) served with a simple tomato sauce, seasoned with the local *piment d'Espelette.*

Les Pâtes au Piment

Pasta with *piment*

4 tbsp best olive oil
½ small dried *piment*, deseeded, finely chopped and pounded (1 tsp of powdered *piment* will substitute well)
2 large ripe tomatoes, peeled and chopped
2 large cloves garlic, finely chopped
salt
350 g pasta
Basque hard cheese (Parmesan will substitute), grated

Warm the oil over a very low heat and add the *piment*. Leave for 15 minutes without allowing it to brown; it should gently colour the oil. Add the tomatoes and mash all together in the pan with the garlic. Season with salt and allow to cook very slowly for 30 minutes. The sauce should be the consistency of a purée.

Cook the pasta in boiling salted water until *al dente.* Drain and serve with the sauce and the grated cheese.

Over to the east, in the Rhône valley, they fabricate pasta in the form of packets of miniature ravioli, which they call *ravioles.* These are simply stuffed with herbs and local cheese. They have spread to the South-West where they can be found in good supermarkets and *épiceries.* Our version makes use of home-grown tarragon, which gives a delicious flavour to the sauce.

Les Ravioles de Romans

Pasta squares stuffed with cheese

4 sprigs of tarragon
1 litre chicken stock (or 1 chicken cube dissolved in water)
5 sheets of ready-made *ravioles de Romans*
4 tbsp crème fraîche
grated hard cheese (*brebis* or Parmesan)

Put the tarragon in a pan with the stock, bring to a boil, then reduce the heat and infuse slowly for 15 minutes. Lower the heat to just below boiling and put in the *ravioles* for just 1 minute– no more. Drain, discarding the tarragon and leaving just a little of the cooking liquid in the bottom with the *ravioles.* Stir in the *crème fraîche*, mix well and serve with the grated cheese.

More often than not, *pâtés* and *terrines* will be based on pork or ham, sometimes prepared with or accompanied by salads or vegetables and served as a first course. Contrast the following simple salad with the more elaborate *terrine* which follows.

La Salade Campagnarde

Country salad

For each person

100 g raw country ham or salt belly of pork, cut in 1-2slices

1 tbsp duck or goose fat

salad vegetables according to season

walnut oil dressing

1 egg

freshly ground pepper

Fry the meat very gently in the fat while you prepare and dress the salad and arrange it on each person's plate.

Put the ham/pork on top of each person's salad, and in the remaining fat, fry the eggs, then use to top the salads. Season with pepper but no salt.

La Terrine Aux Herbes

Herb *pâté*

350 g spinach

350 g raw pork

100 g cooked ham, diced

100 g *lardons*

1 medium onion, finely chopped

½ tbsp each of basil, parsley and chervil

3 rosemary leaves

2 cloves garlic, chopped

cayenne pepper, nutmeg, salt and pepper

2 eggs, lightly beaten

strips of pork fat to line the terrine and cover the *pâté*

Cook the spinach in a pan for 5 minutes, then drain, chop coarsely and mince with the raw pork. Add the ham, *lardons* and onion, then the herbs, garlic and seasonings. Stir in the beaten eggs and turn into a terrine lined with the pork fat. Cover with more strips of the pork fat.

Heat the oven to 150C/300F/gas mark 2. Cover the terrine with foil, put in a *bain-marie* and cook for 1 hour, then allow to cool completely. Serve cold.

Nothing is ever wasted in the South-West. In particular, no part of the duck or goose is allowed to go into the dustbin. Even the innards are preserved under fat like the more choice joints of the birds and form the basis of a delicious *entrée.* This recipe is useful especially in winter when green salads are hard to come by.

La Salade de Noix Aux Gésiers

Salad of walnuts with gizzards

200 g *confit de gésiers* (preserved duck gizzards)
1 head of *endive* (chicory), sliced
3 medium oranges, peeled and sliced
10 walnuts, shelled and broken into pieces
walnut oil dressing

Place the opened tin of *gésiers* in a *bain-marie* or low oven until the fat has melted. Drain off the fat and pat the *gésiers* dry with kitchen paper. Cut them into small cubes.

Arrange some chicory in the centre of each plate and surround with slices of orange. Scatter the chopped *gésiers* and walnut pieces over the chicory and sprinkle with walnut oil dressing just before serving.

o

Eggs have always been a feature of cooking in the South-West – not surprisingly because they cost nothing if the chickens in the farmyard are in laying mood. They form the basis of many a light dish, sometimes as an *entrée* and sometimes as the main course of a meal. The next could be either, and is a staple recipe from the Basque country.

La Pipérade

Omelette of onions, peppers, tomatoes

2 medium-sized onions, chopped
2 tbsp olive oil
3 sweet red or green peppers, de-seeded and cut into rings
500 g ripe tomatoes, peeled and roughly chopped
1 bay leaf
1 tsp chopped thyme
1 piece of fresh or ½ tsp *piment d'Espelette*
salt
1 tsp sugar
4 fairly thin slices *jambon de Bayonne*
4 eggs, beaten as for an omelette

In a large *sauteuse* (sauté pan), melt the onions slowly in the oil but do not let them colour.

Add the peppers, cover with the lid and cook gently, stirring from time to time. After 10 minutes add the remaining ingredients except the eggs and ham, and mix well. Cook everything together for another 15 minutes or until the moisture has sufficiently evaporated.

In a separate frying pan, fry the ham slices gently in oil or butter until softened and the fat is translucent.

Meanwhile, add the eggs to the vegetable mixture, stirring well with a wooden spoon. Cook gently for 1-2 minutes until the eggs are lightly scrambled. They should remain soft and not granulated.

Serve immediately with the ham slices and some country bread.

o

The following, from Aveyron, could hardly be simpler .

Les Oeufs sur le Plat à l'Huile de Noix

Omelette cooked with walnut oil

Per serving
1 slice of bread
garlic
1 tbsp walnut oil
1 egg
filet de vinaigre (*i.e.* a drizzle of vinegar)
2 tsp parsley or chervil, finely chopped

Toast the bread lightly, rub well with garlic while hot and keep in a warm place.

Heat the oil in a small non-stick frying pan; when it is nearly smoking, break the egg into it. Baste continually with the oil. When nearly set, add the vinegar and continue cooking until it has evaporated.

To serve, slide the egg on to the toast, pour over any remaining pan juices and sprinkle with the chopped herbs.

o

It seems that every French person knows how to make the perfect omelette, whether the runny kind favoured by some people nowadays, or the solid type such as the cake-like *auvergnat* Omelette Brayaude (see my earlier book). Not many, however, can expect successfully to serve 130 omelettes at one sitting as did Madame Berthier, the former proprietress of the Lion d'Or at Lalbenque in the Lot.

Lalbenque is the epicentre of truffle production and sales in the South-West. Every Tuesday during the winter, the otherwise unremarkable village is thronged by people from all walks of life–the media, dealers, restaurateurs, tourists or just curious locals–to gaze at the truffles displayed by the local sellers and to taste the results in one of the local cafés. Alas, Madame Berthier is no longer with us, but the omelette tradition continues. Maybe she kept some of her secrets to herself, but the following is what we gathered from her.

L'Omelette Aux Truffes de Madame Berthier

Truffle omelette as made by Mme Berthier

Per person

30 g fresh truffle, brushed, washed and finely chopped
2 eggs
1 knob butter
salt and pepper

Place the chopped truffle in the bottom of a small bowl, break in the eggs and stir gently without beating. Leave to stand in a cool place for 2 hours or more.

Season the mixture and beat it lightly. Heat the butter in a frying pan and make the omelette in the usual way.

Staying for a moment in Lalbenque, the local Office du Tourisme supplied us with a recipe for a delicious *bonne bouche* featuring, of course, the local truffle.

La Truffe en Chausson

Truffle cooked in puff pastry

4 truffles about 15 g (minimum) each
350 g puff pastry
30 g butter
1 egg yolk, beaten
salt

Preheat the oven to 220C/425 F/gas mark 7.

Wash the truffles in running water, using a very soft nail brush to remove any earth clinging to them. Pat them dry.

Roll out the puff pastry to a thickness of 5 mm and cut out 4 circles about 10 cm in diameter. Place a truffle on one half of each circle (cut it in half if necessary in order to fold over the other half and make a complete seal). Before sealing, put a knob of butter on top of the truffle and sprinkle a little salt over. Brush the edges of the pastry with some of the beaten egg yolk, fold over and pinch the two edges together to seal. Use the edge of a knife, 'knock up' the pastry (to allow air in between the layers so it can puff up) and brush the top with more beaten egg.

Place the *chaussons* on a greased baking sheet and bake for 17 minutes until they have risen and are golden and crisp.

Now some treats for vegetarians, not often catered for in a land where meats have traditionally been to the fore in restaurants and celebratory events at home. Today, however, vegetarianism is not only understood but well-catered for in many homes and restaurants.

La Terrine de Chèvre à l'Aubergine

Paté of goats' cheese and aubergine

Serves 8

12 g gelatine leaves
2 long-shaped aubergines
olive oil, for frying
450 g fresh goats' cheese
2 eggs
100 ml crème fraîche
100 ml tomato *coulis*
1 tsp chopped chives, mint, basil
1 tbsp chopped parsley
salt and pepper

Preheat the oven to 180C/350F/gas mark 4.

Soften the gelatine in a bowl of cold water for 5 minutes, then dissolve it in a saucepan with the *crème fraîche* over a gentle flame for 3 minutes. Put aside.

Peel the aubergines and slice each into 3-4 pieces vertically, making little incisions in each. Heat the oil in a pan then fry the aubergines until golden. Drain and put aside.

Put the goats' cheese in a bowl (or blender) with the eggs, *crème fraîche*, herbs and seasonings. Mix thoroughly.

In a *terrine* lined with aluminium foil, put a layer of aubergine covered with half the tomato and half the cheese, then repeat the process, finishing with aubergine. Press down firmly then cook in a *bain-marie* in the oven for 45 minutes.

Allow to cool. Put a layer of clingfilm (or similar) over the *terrine* with a 1 kg weight on top. Leave in a cool place for 6 hours. To serve, unmold the terrine and slice.

La Salade de Riz aux Olives

Rice salad with olives

250 g long white Camargue rice
3 tbsp vinaigrette
2 or 3 small tomatoes, deseeded and cubed
1 green and 1 yellow pepper, deseeded and cubed
3 hard-boiled eggs, sliced
6 canned anchovy fillets, cut into pieces
1½ tbsp capers
110 g whole black olives
salt and pepper

Cook the rice in salted water and drain well. Pour on the vinaigrette, then cover and chill.

Mix the tomatoes and peppers into the chilled rice. Pile on to a large serving dish and decorate with the eggs, anchovies, capers and olives. Season to taste.

An *olivade* is an olive plantation, providing the olives and the olive oil for this recipe.

L'Olivade de Fromage Blanc

Olive and fresh cheese spread

110 g black olives, stoned
1 small onion
250 g fromage blanc
6 tbsp extra virgin olive oil
1 tbsp chopped chives
salt

Crush the olives almost to a purée in a food processor. Chop half the onion finely. Mix the olives into the *fromage blanc*, then slowly stir in half the oil. Add the chopped onion and most of the chives. Turn into a bowl and beat with a wooden spoon, slowly adding the rest of the oil until you have a spreadable mixture. Season to taste. Cover with the remaining half onion cut into rings and a thin layer of oil.

Chill for 24 hours. Remove the onion rings and serve on bread *croutons*, sprinkled with chives.

Every year at the end of October there is a famous chestnut fair at Mourjou in the lower Cantal, the centre of large chestnut plantations. Among the events there will be a cooking competition involving dishes that have to be based on chestnuts. The recipe below featured in the competition one year, and the cook kindly posted the recipe on the door of one of the buildings. A famous guest chef with many Michelin stars must have been in a bad mood because he refused to award a prize that year (he wasn't asked back). I think he was wrong, don't you?

La Terrine de Castanhas

Chestnut pâté

300 g chestnuts in their shells (250 g if already shelled)
1 tbsp sunflower oil
110 g onion, finely chopped
110 g chestnut mushrooms, chopped
6 juniper berries, crushed
pinch of nutmeg
70 g melted butter
salt and pepper

Slit the chestnuts if unshelled then put them in boiling water for 5 minutes. Peel them, removing both inner and outer skins.

Put the nuts into salted water and boil gently for 15 minutes. Drain, blend to a firm purée in a food processor, moistening them with a little water if necessary. Put aside.

Heat the oil in a pan, put in the onion and soften it for five minutes. Add the mushrooms with a little salt. Cover and cook slowly for 10 minutes. Add pepper, the juniper berries and nutmeg, then blend this mixture to a purée in the food processor.

Combine the two mixtures, stir in the melted butter and put it into a *terrine*. Smooth the top and chill. Serve chilled with wholemeal toast.

LA BASSE-COUR

TRADITIONALLY THIS WAS NOT ONLY the part of the farmyard or its adjacent buildings where country families would raise their chickens, geese, ducks and rabbits. *La basse-cour* also meant the activity carried on there, always by the woman of the house. When looking after the geese, she was called *la gardeuse* and features as such on so many old photographs and postcards of the region. She might delegate some of her duties to the children of the family, but the men were not expected or even allowed to interfere.

Today, the *basse-cour* has often morphed into a second *potager*, usually enclosed by a stout wire fence to keep out predators such as foxes. Some may have been acquired from another family or may even continue to be shared with them, already perhaps planted with fruit or nut trees. The larger space permits greater freedom of movement for the livestock, which in turn improves their quality and flavour, reared as they say, *en plein air*.

Of all the produce now normally raised at home, the most important is undoubtedly the chicken, whether it graces the family Sunday lunch or is the centre of a celebratory meal with guests and/or relatives. Its preparation can range from the simplest to the sophisticated, according to the culinary skills of the family. Chicken is easy to prepare in a luxurious way but or quite simply with cream and mushrooms, as below.

Le Poulet à la Crême et Aux Champignons

Chicken legs in mushroom sauce

60 g butter
150 g mushrooms, chopped
2 large shallots, finely chopped
4 cuisses de poulet with the drumsticks
flour, for sprinkling
120 ml white wine
thyme sprigs
bay leaf
6 heaped tbsp crème fraiche
salt and pepper

In a frying pan, melt 30 g of the butter and gently *sauté* the mushrooms and shallots, without browning them, for 15 minutes. Season.

In another pan, melt the rest of the butter and gently brown the chicken pieces all over. Sprinkle with flour and cook gently for 15 minutes. Add the white wine and a little water and let the juices mingle and reduce a little. Season and add the thyme and bay leaf. Turn the chicken pieces over in the pan from time to time, then add the mushroom and shallot mixture and cook gently for 20 minutes.

10 minutes before serving add the cream and stir well, cover the pan and simmer very gently, keeping the dish warm until ready to serve .

Or alternatively you may like the slightly more ambitious version.

Les Cuisses de Poulet, Crême et Champignons

Chicken drumsticks in mushroom sauce

8 tbsp milk
4 heaped tbsp crème fraîche
8 tbsp grated Parmesan cheese
duck or goose fat (or butter)
2 large shallots, thinly sliced
flour, for dusting
4 chicken thighs with drumsticks, or 8 without
300 ml dry white wine
300 g chestnut (or similar) mushrooms, coarsely chopped
pinch of grated nutmeg
knob of butter
salt and pepper

In a small saucepan, stir the milk into the crème fraîche, then add the Parmesan. Mix well until you have a sticky paste. Melt and blend it over a low heat until you have a creamy sauce of good consistency.

Preheat the oven to 350F/180C/gas mark 4. In a heavy frying pan, melt the fat/butter then and the shallots and cook without browning them until translucent. Flour the chicken pieces, add to the pan and cook gently over a low flame for 10 minutes, turning once or twice. Raise the heat and add the wine, reducing it until it has evaporated by half. Transfer all to a gratin dish. Add the mushrooms and seasonings, cover with foil, transfer to the oven and cook for 20 minutes.

Heat the grill to high, remove the dish from the oven, add the pan juices to the cream mixture, mix well and pour all pour over the chicken. Dot with butter and grill for 7 minutes, then reduce the grill to medium and cook for a further 5. Reduce the grill to low and cook for another 5 minutes or until cooked through.

Serve with steamed potatoes. Carrots Vichy sprinkled with parsley make a nice contrast.

Because the thighs and drumsticks of chicken (so much juicier and tastier than the much-vaunted breasts) are so easy to find commercially, there are many variations on how to cook them separately from the rest of the bird. This example does not call for cream but retains the mushrooms. It is one of the many recipes in this book that call for a pan with a tight-fitting lid, indispensable kitchen equipment in the South-West.

Les Quarts de Poulet Braisés

Braised chicken thighs and drumsticks

4 tbsp duck or goose fat
1 onion, cut into rings
200g lardons
250 g mushrooms, roughly chopped
4 chicken thighs with the drumsticks attached
200 ml dry white wine
200 ml water
1 tsp piment d'Espelette
a pinch of dried thyme
salt and pepper

Into a pan with a tight-fitting lid and large enough to take the four chicken pieces in one layer, melt the lardons over a gentle heat and add the onions. When they are soft but not coloured, add the mushrooms and continue cooking gently for 15 minutes. Add the chicken pieces and the wine, the water and seasonings. Cover the pan and continue cooking over a very low flame for 45 minutes, turning the chicken pieces from time to time.

Tarragon has long been a favourite combination with chicken in France. It is easy to grow in our garden, but it spreads quickly and can take over unless frequently cut back (or used in the kitchen). There are two sorts; the Russian kind is much milder than the French variety, which is much to be preferred. The marriage of chicken with tarragon has been celebrated in many forms, from the richest and fanciest *haute cuisine* to more simple ways that do not distract attention from the basic ingredients. For example:

Le Poulet à L'estragon

Chicken legs in tarragon cream sauce

2 tbsp duck or goose fat
4 chicken thighs with their drumsticks
10 sprigs French tarragon
250 ml dry white wine
3 tbsp crème fraîche
salt and pepper

Preheat the oven to 200C/400F/gas mark 6. Heat the fat in a large frying pan and fry the chicken pieces until lightly browned on both sides.

Transfer the chicken to an ovenproof dish large enough to take them in one layer. Pour the wine into the frying pan, bring to the boil and deglaze the pan, scraping up the browned bits from the base. Pour the liquid over the chicken and add half the tarragon sprigs. Cook in the oven for 30 minutes.

Chop the other half of the tarragon finely and add it to the chicken. Keep the dish at simmering point, but no more, while you stir in the crème fraîche and blend the sauce thoroughly. Taste for seasoning.

People in the South-West have generally been shy about exotic spices. Indian food is not, for example, generally to their taste, perhaps because, as a nation, France had only a tiny foothold historically in that country. Nevertheless, with the gradual internationalization of taste, and the preference of the younger generation for spicier food, chicken has not escaped being jazzed up in a mild sort of way.

Le Poulet Aux Épices

Chicken in spice sauce

4 chicken thighs with their drumsticks
3 tbsp best olive oil
1 onion, finely chopped
3 cloves garlic, finely chopped
1 tsp each turmeric, powdered ginger, colombo and cayenne pepper
1 tbsp tomato concentrate
300 ml chicken stock
salt and pepper

Sauté the chicken pieces in the oil, choosing a pan with a good lid and into which the chicken will fit compactly. Let them take colour lightly. Put aside.

In the same oil, soften the onion and garlic without browning them. Add the seasonings and spices and mix well.

Mix the tomato concentrate into the stock and add to the pan. Put back the chicken pieces. Cover and simmer slowly for 40 minutes. Serve with plain rice.

Back to the simple, surprisingly delicious:

Les Cuisses de Poulet au Bouillon

Chicken legs in vegetable stock

2 chicken legs (thighs and drumsticks in one piece)
1 carrot, coarsely chopped
1 medium-sized onion, coarsely chopped
2 cloves garlic, chopped in small cubes
chicken stock
30 g butter
salt and pepper

Put the chicken legs in a casserole just large enough to hold them. Cover with the chopped vegetables, add stock barely to cover and season. Bring to a boil and simmer over low heat for 30 minutes.

Preheat the grill to medium. Remove the chicken pieces from the pot. Melt the butter separately in a small pan and brush the skin of the chicken pieces with it. Season again and grill until crisp and golden.

Meanwhile, reduce the cooking *bouillon* by at least half, strain and serve as a sauce.

o

So much for a bird that has been previously jointed. When cooking a whole bird, one popular family method roasts the chicken on a bed of potatoes, vegetables and/or mushrooms cooking in water with the bird placed dry on the top. The chicken is jointed and served together with the vegetables, which will have absorbed the juices from all the ingredients and have substantially reduced. The quantities are for 4 people, but it is surprising how many portions a skillful carver can achieve with the same quantities.

Le Poulet Rôti Aux Pommes de Terre et Aux Légumes

Roast chicken with potatoes and vegetables

16 small potatoes, unpeeled unless old
12 cloves garlic, peeled but not chopped
2 tbsp duck or goose fat
salt and pepper
1 onion, cut into rings
1 carrot, sliced
1 stick celery, sliced
250 g fresh cèpes (or 60 g dried and reconstituted in a little water) cut into strips or bite-sized pieces
1 farm chicken weighing 2 kg
2 more tbsp duck or goose fat

Preheat the oven to 180C/350 F/gas mark 4. In the bottom of a roasting tin, arrange the potatoes whole with 6 of the garlic cloves and the duck (goose) fat and add 200 ml water. Add the other vegetables and mix all well.

Coat the bird with the rest of the fat and stuff it with the cèpes and the other 6 cloves of garlic. Season well. Put the bird on top of the vegetables and roast for 90 minutes.

No apology is offered for proposing our own way of roasting a chicken whole, which we hope is in the South-Western idiom, but has a few touches of our own.

Le Poulet les Cazes

Roast chicken à Lascazes

1 yellow chicken (*poulet jaune*) about 2 kg with its giblets
tarragon stalks
60 g butter
1 tsp piment d'Espelette
salt
1 tbsp verjus or lemon juice

For the stuffing
1 medium-sized onion
5 to 10 cloves garlic, according to size and taste
handful of tarragon (stalks and leaves)
1 tbsp butter
salt and pepper

Make about 300 ml stock, unseasoned, with the giblets, tarragon stalks and the wing tips from the bird. Simmer for half an hour or more.

Preheat the oven to 220C/400C/gas mark 7. Prepare the stuffing. Cut the onion into six wedges and the garlic into almond-sized pieces, and put these into the chicken's cavity with more tarragon, the 1 tbsp butter and plenty of salt and pepper.

In a bowl or saucer, blend the 60 g butter and the *piment d'Espelette*, coat the chicken with this and season with salt. Roast the bird for 1 hour 20 minutes, adding stock to the pan and basting with the juices every 15 minutes or so. Most will disappear in between bastings.

Transfer to a serving dish and, if the chicken is to be eaten hot, deglaze the pan with the verjuice or lemon juice, and serve the juices as gravy. If the bird is to be eaten cold, joint it on to a serving platter and decorate with the garlic stuffing.

Coq au vin has become something of a *cliché* as well as a standby dish, and one that some people try to simplify to a basic level. Not so Madame Issaly, the *mamie* of the Domaine de la Ramaye at Gaillac, where the family make some of the finest wines of that region. This is not surprising when they have been brought up on the sumptuous cooking of the lady of the house. You will need perseverance to find an appropriate cockerel, and sufficient patience (three days) and stamina to devote to its preparation for the table. Both are infinitely worth it.

Le Vieux Coq de la Ramaye

Cockerel as cooked at the Domaine de Ramaye

Serves 6-8

3 kg cockerel 2 years old or so
80 g duck or goose fat
5 cloves garlic
2 leeks, cut in thin rounds
3 carrots, sliced
3 medium-sized onions
200 g fresh belly of pork, chopped
100 g salt back pork
50 ml Armagnac
1 bottle each of dry white wine and good red
120 ml strong black coffee
250 g small young *cèpes* or other wild mushrooms, coarsely chopped
thyme sprigs and parsley leaves
50 peppercorns
salt
8 croûtons country bread
salt and pepper

Day One
Joint the bird into serving pieces. In a large pan, brown them lightly in the duck or goose fat for 5 minutes on each side and set them aside.

Grease a large, enamelled *marmite*. Brown the vegetables gently in the same pan, add both types of pork, pour in the

Armagnac and *flamber* . In a separate large pan, bring the two wines to a boil. Flame it for a few seconds, then suppress the flames with the lid.

In the *marmite*, spread the cockerel on the bed of vegetables and pork. Sprinkle in the coffee. Bring all back to the boil and pour in the wine. Add the mushrooms. Season with the herbs peppercorns and salt. Cover and allow to simmer very gently for 1½ hours. Leave overnight in the cellar or other cool place.

Day Two

Put the *marmite* back on a very low heat, bringing it barely to the simmer and cover. An hour and a half from cold will suffice. Put it back in the cellar.

Day Three

Skim the fat from the surface of the *marmite* and put it aside. Put the *marmite* back on the lowest possible heat covered for another two hours .

Just before serving, spread some of the reserved fat on the croûtons and grill them.

To serve the bird, remove the pieces to a large serving-dish. Pour the sauce over it. (There ought to be about 650 ml of sauce; if there is more, reduce it.) Arrange the croutons around the chicken pieces.

o

Although the goose, increasingly seldom to be found, is undoubtedly the monarch of the *basse-cour*, its place is gradually being usurped by the duck, which is easier to rear, needing only two feeds instead of the three called for the goose when it is prepared for the ultimate sacrifice. Whole ducks are not very often seen even at market, because the bird so easily joints itself into manageable pieces with which to make *confit*. This is abundantly sold *sous-vide*, which enables the consumer to keep the packets for weeks at a time, and, coming from a reputable source, can be nearly as good as *confit* made at home and preserved under its own fat.

Ever since the famous chef André Daguin from Auch introduced the *magret* to the world in 1965 (he says he recovered it from memories of his childhood and did not invent it), it has become a mainstay of the South-West repertoire. Chefs have invented many variations on the cooking and presentation of a *magret*, sometimes with honey, otherwise with a *compote* of apples. But to us nothing beats André's simple method and we add some words of advice of our own.

Magret de Canard

Fattened duck breast

1. Score the fat side crosswise several times with a sharp knife, cutting the fat down to but not through the flesh below.
2. Be generous with the seasoning, especially salt, which should be rubbed carefully into the fat.
3. We like to give the *magret* a preliminary marinade for a couple of hours with bay leaves, thyme, seasonings (including a little *piment d'Espelette)* and 2 tbsp of Armagnac.
4. Be sure to allow as much of the fat to run before cooking the *magret*. We find that putting it in a warm oven (70C/150F) for 45 minutes will yield a surprisingly large amount of beautiful duck fat, which you can use to cook any accompanying potatoes - *pommes de terre rissolées* for example (page 112), which go wonderfully well with a *magret.*
5. Remember that a *magret* is not a *magret* at all unless it comes from a duck fattened by *gavage*. It is otherwise just a breast of duck, and it will not have the necessary overcoat of fat.

There are, however, less well-known ways of dealing with the rest of the bird. The legs can be prepared from raw in this unusual Gascon way.

Les Cuisses de Canard au Madiran

Duck legs cooked in Madiran wine

4 tbsp duck or goose fat
4 duck legs
200 g *lardons*/green (unsmoked) streaky bacon in cubes
4 shallots, finely chopped
4 cloves garlic, finely chopped
flour, for dusting
1 bottle of Madiran or other sturdy red wine
2 chicken stock cubes, crumbled
2 sprigs of thyme
4 bay leaves
1 tsp quatre épices
2 tbsp redcurrant jelly
salt and pepper

In a *cocotte*, heat the duck fat and sear the duck legs on both sides, transfer to a warm place and drain off most off the fat.

In the fat remaining, sweat the shallots, garlic and lardons until softened but not coloured. Put back the duck legs and sprinkle generously with flour. Add the wine and the stock cubes, the thyme, bay leaves, spice and seasonings, bring to the boil and leave to simmer very gently, covered, for 2 ½ hours, turning the duck legs halfway through. The liquid should just about cover the duck.

Remove the duck legs to a warm place. Strain the juices into a small pan, putting the solids with the duck. Add the redcurrant jelly to the sauce and reduce by half; serve separately.

Good with bitter greens; mashed potatoes too.

Duck also lends itself to mild spicing, as in the following recipe for a tagine. Tagines are quite commonly found in the larger cities of the South-West, where the immigrant population in particular like to revive memories of home. The quantities are given for 2 people, because not many have a true Moroccan *tagine* big enough for four. For four people just double up the quantities and cook in a wide *cocotte* with a tight-fitting lid.

Les Cuisses de Canard en Tagine

A tagine of duck legs

Serves 2

2 duck legs and thighs
salt and pepper
1 medium-sized onion, sliced in rings
3 cloves garlic, roughly chopped
1 tsp ground cinnamon
1 tsp ground ginger
1 tsp ras-el-hanout
good pinch of saffron, crushed in a mortar
750 ml duck or chicken stock
6 dried apricots, pre-soaked
6 prunes, pre-soaked
2 tbsp toasted almonds

Prick the fat of the duck pieces all over without piercing the flesh, and roast at 220C/425F/gas 7 for 45 minutes.

Meanwhile, in a casserole with a tight-fitting lid, *sauté* gently the sliced onion , garlic and all the spices in 1½ tbsp of the fat that will have run from the duck. Do not brown. Set aside until the duck legs are done, then transfer the duck to the casserole and add the stock.

Simmer slowly for an hour covered, add the apricots and the prunes and continue simmering for another half hour.

Serve with couscous, sprinkled with the toasted almonds.

The part of the duck that corresponds to the *suprême* of a chicken is called *aiguillette*, quite narrow strips of flesh from the part of the breast nearest the bone which are detached from the *magret* before the latter is sold or packaged. The *aiguillette* is quite distinct from the *magret*, which is removed from the carcass, leaving the *aiguillette* behind. They need very little cooking, like their chicken counterparts, and are popular for that reason. This version combines the sweetness of cherries with shallot and pepper.

Les Aiguillettes de Canard Aux Echalotes et Aux Cérises

Duck *aiguillettes* with shallots and cherries

3 shallots, finely chopped
600 g *aiguillettes de canard*
250 g cherries, stoned and halved
1 tsp piment d'Espelette
salt and pepper

Heat the duck fat in a heavy-based pan, then add the shallots and gently cook until golden and melted. Add the *aiguillettes,* season and cook briskly for 2 minutes on each side. Remove and set aside in a warm place.

In the same pan, add the cherries and cook over a low heat, letting them melt a little, stirring well. Put back the *aiguillettes*, add the *piment*, mix well and serve.

The South-West is prune country *par excellence*, so it is not surprising that ways have been found of marrying the fruit with duck. This is an attractive way of serving both, combining the richness of the bird with the sweetness of the prunes.

Les Aiguillettes de Canard Aux Pruneaux

Duck *aiguillettes* with prunes

400 ml red wine
6 tbsp prune juice
2 heaped tsp honey
600 g aiguillettes de canard
as many prunes, whole, as there are aiguillettes
4 tbsp duck or goose fat
salt and pepper
verjus (or lemon juice)

To make the sauce, put the wine, prune juice and honey in a saucepan, stir well and put over a low flame to reduce until syrupy.

Meanwhile, roll up a prune in each of the *aiguillettes* and secure with toothpicks. Season.

Heat the fat in a pan and sauté the *aiguillettes* briefly, turning them over to ensure even cooking, keeping them pink. Transfer to a serving dish, deglaze the pan with the *verjus* (or lemon juice) and add the pan juices to the sauce.

Serve with *pommes rissolés* and a green salad or vegetable.

In the Roussillon, where cherries are grown with such success for export all over France, and where the fortified wine of Banyuls is a great favourite, it is not surprising that they have evolved a way of cooking duck that explores their local produce.

Le Canard Aux Cérises et au Vieux Banyuls

Duck with cherries and Banyuls wine

1 duck for roasting
2 tbsp duck or goose fat
12 button onions
1 medium-sized onion, chopped
1 heaped tsp flour
400 ml stock
200 ml Banyuls wine
1 bouquet garni
120 g dark cherries
coarse salt and pepper

Prick the skin of the duck all over without piercing the flesh, and rub it with plenty of salt and pepper. Roast it at 200C/375F/gas mark 6 for 45 minutes. When cool enough, joint into 8 pieces.

Meanwhile, blanch the button onions. In a casserole, heat the fat, then soften the blanched onions and the chopped onion. Thicken with the flour and dilute with the stock. Add 120 ml of the Banyuls wine. Put the duck legs in the bottom of the casserole, add the *bouquet garni* and simmer gently for 25 minutes. Add the breasts and continue cooking for 15 minutes. Transfer the duck pieces and the button onions to a dish and keep warm, then educe the casserole juices.

Put the cherries in a small pan with the remaining Banyuls and simmer gently for 5 minutes. With a slotted spoon, drain the cherries and arrange round the duck. Strain the casserole juices through a sieve into the cherry liquor and serve separately.

Les Manchons de Canard

Duck wings

The *manchon* is the first joint of the wing of the duck. It is much used in the making of *cassoulets* and other slow-cooked recipes but can be enjoyed also *en confit*. It is easily bought pre-packed and can be quickly prepared in a frying pan, with or without extra ingredients. A good sauce can, however, add to its interest so here are two:

1. Soften some shallots in duck fat in a frying pan with the manchons, adding diced oranges confites, capers, and a little red wine to make a short sauce after bubbling it up for few seconds.
2. "Medieval" is the word given to describe a sauce recipe given to us locally. Chop and pound 4 cloves of garlic with a little salt. Mix in 50 g grated ewes' milk cheese, 3 tbsp olive oil and 3 tbsp sunflower oil, a handful of chopped basil leaves and pepper.

The third mainstay of the *basse-cour* is the rabbit, a fast-disappearing animal in the natural habitat because of the use of chemicals and artificial fertilisers in the fields. The domestically reared rabbit is, however, a fair substitute and far preferable to the pre-packed carcasses to be found in the supermarkets. The methods of preparation are relatively simple, the most basic of all is to roast it over your open fire and baste it with pork fat in your *flambadou*. But, with the gradual disappearance of open fireplaces, this may not be feasible. Variations within the regions of the South-West are to be expected. For example, a delightful neighbour who used to help us in the house, gave us this version:

Le Lapin Vivianne

Rabbit à la Vivianne

3 tbsp olive oil
1 rabbit, jointed
200 g unsmoked *lardons*
2 large onions, cut in rings
2 tbsp flour
250 g button mushrooms
250 ml dry white wine
250 ml water
salt and pepper

In a *cocotte* with a tight-fitting lid, heat the oil and brown the rabbit pieces over a good heat, reserving the liver (which takes less time to cook). Remove the rabbit pieces while you brown the *lardons* and the onions in the oil. Put back the rabbit pieces and flour them, stirring vigorously. Season generously.

Add the wine gradually, then the water and finally the mushrooms.

Reduce the heat and simmer for 30 minutes. Add the liver cut into good chunks and cook another 30 minutes. Serve with plain rice or steamed potatoes.

Mustard gives some oomph to the rather delicate flavour of rabbit. There are many ways of combining the two, but the following is typical.

Le Lapin à la Moutarde

Rabbit in a mustard sauce

1 rabbit, jointed
200 ml crème fraîche
2 tbsp grainy French mustard
salt and pepper

100 ml Banyuls wine
2 tbsp chopped tarragon
salt and pepper

Preheat the oven to 240C/460F/gas mark 8.

Put the rabbit pieces in a *gratin* dish in a single layer without overlapping. Put all but 1 tbsp of the crème fraîche into a bowl with the mustard and some salt. Mix well. Coat the rabbit pieces with this mixture, cook them in the oven for 40 minutes, then put aside and keep warm.

Rinse out the *gratin* dish with the Banyuls and pour into a small saucepan. Boil hard for 2 minutes. Add the last tablespoon of the cream, some pepper and the tarragon. Stir together over a low flame for 3 minutes, coat the rabbit with the sauce and serve.

Mushrooms are another favourite partner for rabbit. For this recipe, use cèpes if you can, but any wild variety will do.

Le Lapin Bonne Femme

Rabbit with mushrooms

1 rabbit
300 g mushrooms
4 tbsp duck or goose fat
100 g salt belly of pork (thick slices of green (unsmoked) streaky bacon will do), cubed
12 pickling onions, peeled
2 tbsp crème fraîche
2 tbsp chopped parsley
salt and pepper

Joint the rabbit, wipe the mushrooms clean and cut them into quarters or thick slices if they are large.

In a heavy-bottomed *cocotte*, brown the rabbit pieces in half the fat. Remove and put aside. Add the remaining fat to the pan and fry the mushrooms, pork and onions over a brisk heat for 5 minutes. Return the rabbit pieces to the pan, moisten with 100 ml of water and season the dish. Cover with a tight-fitting lid and allow to simmer slowly for 45 minutes.

Incorporate the cream and the parsley and increase the heat under the *cocotte* for a few minutes before serving. Steamed potatoes are all you will need.

Garlic is never far away from South-West cooking, and rabbit does not escape its attraction. The pink garlic from Lautrec is best for the next dish, although it is not available until July. In the earlier part of the year use the violet or white garlic, which are what you will find in the markets. Supermarket garlic (usually imported from far away) is not as good.

Le Lapin en Cocotte à l'Ail

Rabbit cooked with garlic

1 rabbit
1 tbsp olive oil
40 (yes, 40) cloves garlic, unpeeled
a good handful of parsley, finely chopped
salt and pepper

Joint the rabbit and put to fry gently in a *cocotte* with the oil. When the pieces have taken on colour, add a glass of water, season and add the garlic. Cover and leave to cook gently for 40 minutes.

Add the parsley and serve the rabbit with the garlic cloves still unpeeled (*en chemise*).

A few people still keep guinea fowl, but not many because of the awful noise the birds make. They are, however, a delightful change from chicken, slightly more gamey although they tend to be dry unless prepared in a way that preserves or creates moisture. For this reason, we prefer cooking them *en cocotte* rather than roasting them in the oven.

La Pintade en Cocotte

Guinea fowl cooked *en cocotte*

4 medium-sized potatoes, quartered
4 large carrots, peeled and chopped
2 medium-sized onions, peeled and chopped
1 tbsp butter
2 tbsp olive oil
1 dsp herbes de Provence
1 tsp ground cumin
1 tbsp salt
1½ tsp piment d'Espelette
1 guinea fowl (about 1.5 kg)
120 ml dry white wine

Preheat the oven to 220C/425F/gas mark 7.

Put the vegetables in the bottom of a large lidded ovenproof *cocotte*. Add the butter oil, herbs and cumin, season with the salt and *piment d'Espelette* and mix all together. Add the bird and stir it round with the vegetables and seasonings so as to coat the bird as far as possible.

Cover the *cocotte*, put it in the oven and reduce the temperature to 180C/350F/gas mark 4. Cook for just under 1 hour.

Add the white wine and cook for another 15 minutes. Remove from the heat and leave to stand for another 15 minutes. Transfer the bird to a carving board, carve and serve with the rest of the contents of the *cocotte* separately.

Pigeons have a long history in the South-West; not the wild kind that wake you in the morning with their ridiculous song, nor the beautiful turtle doves that still adorn our woods and are protected. We are here concerned with the very special birds that are reared specifically for the table. Especially after the Revolution, the ownership of a *pigeonnier* either as a separate building or as an integral part of the farmhouse became a status symbol, and the fertiliser obtained from the birds was for long the only kind allowed in some of the vineyards. The birds themselves were as carefully looked after as the rest of the *basse-cour* and became famous for the succulence and flavour of their meat.

Unless you have your own *pigeonnier* and breed your own, you may find it difficult to find pigeons for the table anywhere except at market. Butchers rarely have them and supermarkets never. But if you are lucky enough to find some, they make marvellous eating, whether plainly roasted with plenty of fat to keep them moist, or, like so many dishes in this book, cooked *en cocotte*.

Les Pigeons en Cocotte au vin Doux (For 2)

Pigeons cooked in sweet wine

150 g lardons
2 tbsp duck or goose fat
2 pigeons with their livers (a prized delicacy)
2 cloves garlic, cut in half
1 medium-sized onion, cut into rings
120 ml sweet wine such as Banyuls
250 ml chicken stock
salt and pepper

In a *cocotte* with a good lid, soften the *lardons* in the fat, then brown the birds on all sides. Set them aside while you soften but not brown the garlic and onions. Put the birds back in the *cocotte* and pour the wine and stock over. Season. Bring back to simmering point, cover and leave to cook gently for 40 minutes, basting the birds from time to time.

Steamed potatoes and *petits pois* are a good accompaniment.

LES POISSONS

FOR SUCH A HUGE COUNTRY, France has the most sophisticated fish-distribution system you can find perhaps anywhere in Europe. Although the number of smaller fish-mongers in the country towns of the South-West is shrinking, this is due to the intense competition of the supermarkets, where the range and freshness of the fish is astonishing. Even in our local village we can buy langoustines, mussels, salt cod, salmon and a variety of fish fillets from monkfish, cod, sea bass and the cheaper *lieu.* The larger cities also have markets, where whole sections are given over to fish: at the Victor Hugo covered market in Toulouse, for example, there were at the last count no fewer than 12 fish retailers who were able to draw on the varied resources of both the Atlantic and Mediterranean waters. Here the variety of shell-fish is astonishing, the small *bouchots* clamouring for attention from the larger more familiar variety: clams, sea snails (*bulots*), prawns and shrimps of all varieties and size, and langoustines whose size dictates their price. The following recipe for the baby mussels is typical of the way they prepare them in Bordeaux.

Les Moules à la Bordelaise

Mussels as prepared in Bordeaux

2 kg *bouchot* mussels
60 g butter
70 g shallots, chopped
4 tomatoes, peeled, de-seeded and finely chopped
300 ml dry white wine
3 tbsp fresh breadcrumbs
½ tsp piment d'Espelette
2 tbsp chopped parsley

Scrub and debeard the mussels under running water, discarding any that are slightly open.

Melt half the butter in a pan, add the shallots and soften over a gentle heat. Mix in the tomatoes then set aside.

Place the mussels in a large pan with the wine. Cover and place over a high heat for a few minutes, shaking the pan. As soon as the mussels start to open, take the pan off the heat and remove the empty half shells of each, placing the full shells in a large serving bowl. Keep warm in a very low oven while finishing the sauce.

Strain the liquid from the mussels into the shallot and tomato mixture, stir in the breadcrumbs, the *piment* and the remaining butter, cut into small cubes.

Reheat gently then spoon the sauce over the mussels, sprinkle with parsley and serve.

Oyster sellers can draw on the extensive beds at Arcachon not far away to the West. Oysters are a regular feature of even quite modest households on feast days such as New Year's Eve: strange, because you will find it hard to buy an oyster in London at any time between Christmas Eve and the middle of January when our fishermen seem to pack up altogether. Usually the French will eat them just as they are, perhaps with a little chopped shallot, vinegar or both, but more adventurous souls find the following recipe both simple and suitably festive.

Les Huîtres au Gratin

Oysters cooked with cheese topping

24 oysters, shucked and put into the larger half of their shells
110 g fresh breadcrumbs
4 tbsp milk
5 shallots, finely chopped
salt and pepper
200 g grated cheese (Cantal or Cheddar)

Preheat the oven to 230C/450F/gas mark 8.

Arrange the oysters in their shells in a shallow *gratin* dish large enough to hold them in one layer. Soak the breadcrumbs in the milk and add the shallots. Cover the tops of the oysters with this mixture. Season, allowing for the saltiness of the cheese which you now sprinkle over the oysters. Bake the dish in the oven for 7 minutes or so until the cheese starts to crisp.

Serve piping hot with *pain de campagne* and a chilled white wine.

Scallops are another favourite, sold sometimes in their shells and sometimes without them. In Provence they are usually eaten briefly fried in olive oil with plenty of garlic and parsley. Further west, mushrooms are a favourite partner.

Les Noix de Saint-Jacques Aux Champignons

Scallops fried with mushrooms

16 fresh scallops
olive oil for frying
400 g chestnut mushrooms, halved or quartered according to size
4 tsp fresh thyme leaves
2 large cloves garlic, finely chopped
salt and pepper
chopped parsley, to serve

Cut the scallops into suitable pieces (corals and white flesh separated).

Heat a little oil in a frying pan over a good flame and cook the mushrooms, stirring. Add the thyme and stir well. Add the whites of the scallops and a little more oil, searing them quickly for a couple of minutes on each side. At the last moment add the corals and cook briefly. Sprinkle with parsley and serve.

o

The natives of the Camargue used to travel the long way to Bordeaux to buy their cod, which they paid for using their home-farmed salt as a means of currency. They would use salt to preserve the cod, a technique that has become widespread all over the south. It is called *morue.* (It should be noted that *morue* is not at all the same as stockfish which forms the basis of the Aveyronnais *estofinado* and which is wind-dried and not salted.) Of the many ways of preparing *morue,* one of the best comes from where it was invented. The contrast between the lightly salted cod and the sweetness of the leeks is excellent.

La Quinquebine

Salt cod cooked with onions and leeks

450 g salt cod (soaked in water overnight)
4 tbsp olive oil
2 onions, sliced
4 leeks, including the green parts, cut vertically into 2.5cm pieces
2 cloves garlic, crushed
3 bay leaves
1 sprig of thyme
freshly ground black pepper

Rinse and drain the fish and place in a pan of cold water. Bring it almost to the boil and poach it for 5 minutes. Drain, then remove and discard the skin and bones. Flake the flesh.

Heat the oil in a lidded casserole, add the onions and the leeks, cover and allow to cook gently for 10 minutes until they are softened but not coloured.

Stir in the flaked fish, the garlic and herbs and continue cooking for 5 minutes. Season with black pepper before serving.

Wild salmon is as rare and expensive in France as anywhere, but it has always been a popular fish. Supplies nowadays will usually be farmed and are widely available in the supermarkets. In smoked form, it is not as un-French as might be thought, because the smoking of food is such a long tradition in the French countryside. The following is an attractive way of using salmon in both its guises as an *entrée.*

Les Poissons Roses à l'Aneth

Salmon and prawns with dill

Serves 6-8

500 g fresh salmon (skinned and filleted)
250 g smoked salmon
125 g shelled prawns
salt and pepper

For the sauce
3 tbsp Dijon mustard
2 tbsp sugar
2 tbsp white wine vinegar
4-5 tbsp olive oil
2 tbsp mixed and chopped dill, parsley and chives
1 lemon or lime

Cut the salmon into small cubes.

For the sauce, mix the mustard with the sugar and vinegar, then beat in the oil to make a thick vinaigrette. Stir in the herbs, reserving some dill for the garnish. Check the seasoning, varying the sweet and sour flavour to taste. Fold in the salmon cubes and prawns. Chill in the refrigerator until required.

To serve, take a strip of smoked salmon about 6 inches long and 2½ to 3 inches wide. Place 1 tbsp of the fish mixture on one end and roll it up. Serve on a bed of lettuce, decorated with a little more dill, and a slice of lemon or lime.

There seems to be an erosion in the number of lorry drivers and other working people who take time off for an old-fashioned two-hour lunch. Employers, particularly those in the remoter country areas, sometimes provide a quick snack on location, perhaps to avoid encroachment on working hours. Sébastien Balard and his wife Christine nevertheless maintain the lunch tradition at their delightful restaurant close to our home. In addition, they also provide more elaborate menus for weekenders and tourists, for whom they have elaborated and shared with us the following fragrant summer salad, which can be taken either as an *entrée* for 4 or as a *plat* for 2.

Le Saumon Fumé et les Crevettes en Salade

Salad of smoked salmon and prawns

2 small flat peaches (*pêches plates*), blanched, skinned and cut into small dice
1 apricot, blanched, skinned and cut into small dice
1 lemon
crispy lettuce
16 prawns, precooked
4 slices smoked salmon
a good pinch each of cayenne pepper and *piment d'Espelette*
6 tbsp best olive oil

Divide the peaches and apricot between 2 (or 4) serving bowls. Cut off the top of the lemon, chop into small dice and add to the bowls with the lettuce, cut into convenient pieces.

Shell the prawns and add to the bowls with the slices of smoked salmon, cut into smaller pieces if desired. In a small jug, squeeze the juice from the lemon. Add both types of pepper, then the oil and stir well.

Divide the dressing between the bowls and toss together well.

Quiches are found all over France and are a popular standby, particularly as a snack meal for the young. Made with smoked salmon, they become something rather special. You do not need the expensive cuts of the fish; the trimmings will do just as well.

La Quiche au Saumon Fumé

Smoked salmon quiche

Serves 6-8

For a 25-28cm flan case:
butter for greasing
500 g good quality store-bought puff pastry
18 g smoked salmon
250 ml whipping cream
4-5 eggs according to size
salt, pepper and grated nutmeg

Preheat the oven to 220C/425 F/gas mark 7.

Roll out the pastry and use it to line the buttered flan case. Cut up the salmon into small pieces. Beat the eggs and blend in the cream. Season, being careful with the salt. Mix in the salmon pieces and pour into the pastry case.

Bake the quiche for 15 minutes. Reduce the heat a little to 200C/400F/gas mark 6 for a further 15 minutes or until nicely risen and golden on the top.

With the increasing popularity of rice from the Camargue, it is not surprising that the French have also acquired a taste for risotto, though of course it should be made not with the native rice but the special Italian risotto rice. It is important in the recipe below that you cook the prawns yourself because their stock is such an important feature in the flavour of the finished dish.

Le Risotto de Crevettes

Prawn risotto

Serves 2

12 raw prawns (more or fewer, depending on size)
1 vegetable stock cube
3 tbsp olive oil
1 large or 2 small shallots, finely chopped
100 ml dry white wine
200 g risotto rice
salt and pepper

Put the prawns in a saucepan and cover barely with water. Add the vegetable stock cube. Bring to a simmer and cook gently for 7 minutes.

Transfer the prawns to a board and shell them, tipping the shells back into the water in which they were cooked. Chop the prawns into small pieces.

Bring the shells and their liquid back to a boil and simmer for 20 minutes. Drain, discarding the shells and preserving the liquid, into which you tip the chopped prawns, and keep over a very low heat while you make the risotto.

Heat the oil and melt the shallots without letting them colour. Add the white wine, rice and mix well. Cover generously with the prawn stock and cook the risotto in the usual way, adding the stock as required. 10 minutes before serving, add the chopped prawns, season to taste and serve when the risotto has achieved the desired texture.

Tuna is fished in large quantities from both the Atlantic and Mediterranean, and is often eaten cold in salads as well as hot. Bluefin tuna from the Atlantic is highly prized, can grow to 2 feet long and live, it is said, for up to 50 years. Firm of flesh, it is well-suited to slow cooking in a casserole.

My good friend Erick Vedel from Arles has kindly supplied a *Provençal* interpretation, a far cry from the Basque stew called *marmitako*, in which the locals celebrate their red peppers and the fiery *piment d'Espelette* as well as the more conventional tomatoes and potatoes.

Le Thon à la Chartreuse

Tuna with Chartreuse

700 g fresh tuna
2 tbsp extra virgin olive oil
200 g onion, halved and sliced
500 g tomatoes, each cut into 8 segments
½ lemon, thinly sliced
2 dried bay leaves, crumbled
1 small red chilli, halved and deseeded
200 ml dry white wine
salt and pepper

Preheat the oven to 180C/350F/gas mark 4.

Skin and bone the fish and cut into slices 2.5cm thick.

Coat the bottom of a casserole with the oil and spread a third of the onions over it, followed by slices of tuna and some of the tomatoes, more onion, some of the lemon slices and the bay leaves. Add a second layer of tuna and the rest of the dry ingredients. Pour in the white wine and top up with just enough water to cover the fish.

Cover and bring to the boil over a medium heat, then transfer the casserole to the oven and cook for about 1 hour until the fish is cooked. Test for seasoning during the cooking. This dish can be eaten hot or cold.

A cold fish *entrée* does much to make life more convenient for the cook, especially when it can be prepared ahead of time. Here is a local version of a favourite way of making a fish terrine, given to us by a local farmer's wife who obviously knows a thing or two about cooking.

Le Pain de Poisson

Fish terrine

250 g filleted salmon
250 g other fish (cod or coley perhaps)
1 litre court bouillon
75 g breadcrumbs
100 ml milk
2 large or 3 small eggs
35 g tomato concentrate
1 small onion, finely chopped
a few peeled shrimps (optional)
3 tbsp chopped parsley
salt and pepper
mayonnaise, to serve

Preheat the oven to 190C/375F/gas mark 5.

Poach the fish for 12 minutes in the *court bouillon*. Lift out, drain and remove and discard any skin. Break up the fish into small pieces. Soak the breadcrumbs in the milk, drain them if necessary and mix them with the fish.

In a bowl, beat the eggs with some salt and pepper and the tomato concentrate. Mix this with the fish, adding the finely chopped onion. Check the seasoning and pour the mixture into a buttered ovenproof terrine dish (preferably rectangular to make for easier slicing when served). Cook in a *bain-marie* in the oven for 40 minutes.

Leave to cool before turning out, and decorate with a few shrimps (if used) and some chopped parsley. Serve with mayonnaise.

This fish terrine can be prepared in advance and will keep covered for 48 hours in the refrigerator.

This cold fish *entrée* requires a very sharp knife and some skill in wielding it. Trout has always been a favourite fish in the South-West, although the restrictions on fishing for it has resulted in most of it coming from specialized trout farms. At Lautrec, it is not difficult to imagine the urge to combine trout with the very special garlic of that area, and this recipe comes from the *patron* at the Auberge Le Garde Pile. It calls for an unusually large fish weighing about 1.5 kg.

Il Carpaccio de Truite à l'Ail Rose de Lautrec

Carpaccio of trout with the pink Lautrec garlic

1 large trout
2 tbsp crushed redcurrants
3 cloves Lautrec garlic, chopped
salt
2 lemons, juice
100 ml best olive oil

Remove the fins and bones from the trout. With a large well-sharpened knife, carve fine slices from the fish and put them in a serving dish, not touching each other. Sprinkle over the garlic and the redcurrants, season and pour over the lemon juice and oil. Can be eaten immediately or kept to marinate in the refrigerator for up to 2 hours.

Garlic features in many fish recipes in the Midi, perhaps one of the best-known being *L'Aïoli*, a term that requires some explanation. Often it is used simply to denote a garlic-flavoured mayonnaise to accompany a variety of dishes, cold meats included. It also gives its name to a version of poached fish; one relatively simple being an ordinary Friday dish, the other a more festive affair traditionally served on important feast days.

L'Aïoli

Garlic mayonnaise

Serves 8

For the garlic mayonnaise
6-8 cloves garlic, crushed with a little salt
4 egg yolks
600 ml best olive oil
lemon juice (optional)

For the 'ordinary' aïoli
1 kg *morue* (salt cod), soaked in water for 24 hours
1 kg waxy new potatoes, unpeeled
750 g young carrots, cut into lengths

For the 'grand' Aöli', as above plus all or any of the following
24 canned snails
4-6 hard-boiled eggs
450 g haricots verts
1 cauliflower, divided into florets
8 tiny artichokes
450 g beetroot

First prepare the mayonnaise. All the ingredients must be at room temperature. In a bowl, whisk the garlic and egg yolks, then start adding the oil, a very little at a time, beating continuously. Only when the aïoli begins to thicken can the oil be added more steadily. It should become very thick. Add a little lemon juice if wished. If the mayonnaise curdles, begin again in a clean bowl with another egg yolk, and trickle in the curdled sauce drop by drop, beating all the time.

The accompanying fish and vegetables should be served slightly warm. Poach the fish for 5 minutes. Heat the snails in their liquid and drain. Steam or boil the vegetables, keeping the potatoes in their skins. Arrange portions of the fish and each of the vegetables in separate serving dishes and pass the bowl of aïoli separately. A cool rosé wine is a recommended accompaniment.

Sea bass is one of the most esteemed of all fishes, a favourite at all levels of society even though it is not cheap. Having bought one from our local fishmonger, we took it home and searched among our food supplies to get some ideas of how to cook it. We came up with the following, which works surprisingly well.

Le Loup de Mer Avec les Poireaux et le Fenouil

Sea bass with leeks and fennel

1 sea bass weighing about 1 kg
2 tbsp mixed chopped parsley and chervil
2 heads fennel, thinly sliced (discard the outer tough layers), 1 tbsp of the chopped leaves reserved
2 slices fresh ginger
2 tbsp olive oil, plus extra for greasing
2 medium-sized leeks, finely sliced
2 heads of fennel
2 cloves garlic, finely chopped
salt and pepper

Ask your fishmonger to gut the sea bass but leave the head on. Clean it, fill the cavity with a mixture of the chopped herbs, fennel leaves and ginger and season lightly.

Preheat the oven to 190C/375F/gas mark 5.

Thinly slice the fennel bulbs and blanch for 3 minutes. Drain.

Oil a large sheet of aluminium foil, spread over the fennel and leeks with the garlic on it and put the fish on top. Pour some olive oil over and add more seasoning.

Seal up the foil around the fish, place on a baking tray in the centre of the oven and bake for 25 minutes.

Serve with steamed potatoes dressed in parsley butter.

Another very popular fish in the South-West is the monkfish (*lotte*), so popular, in fact, that every region seems to have its own particular way of cooking it, whether in red wine, and/or with mushrooms; with red peppers in the Roussillon or white wine and Armagnac in Gascony. No apologies are therefore needed for including four recipes for this fish.

When buying *lotte*, ask the fishmonger to skin and fillet the fish, which is otherwise a rather tiresome task. The skin and bones will account roughly for a quarter of the raw fish.

This is how you might find *lotte* in the Bordelais.

La Lotte au vin Rouge de St-Émilion

Monkfish cooked in red wine from St-Emilion

2 tbsp olive oil
12 pickling onions, peeled
2 tsp sugar
150 g salt belly of pork, diced
2 large onions, sliced
4 cloves garlic, finely chopped
3 shallots, chopped
salt and pepper
pinch each of cayenne pepper and *quatre-épices*
bouquet garni, if possible including fennel leaves
4 tbsp flour
25 g butter
1 bottle St-Émilion or other good red wine
250 g *cèpes* or other mushrooms, sliced
2 monkfish tails weighing 400 g each, boned and cut into 2.5cm cubes
croutons of fried bread or puff pastry *fleurons* (optional)
salt and pepper

Heat the oil in a pan, add the pickling onions and cook slowly for 20 minutes, sprinkling with the sugar halfway through, so that they take on a little colour. Add the pork, sliced onions, garlic, shallots, seasonings and *bouquet garni.*

In another pan, over a medium heat, make a roux with the flour and butter and gradually add the wine, stirring until smooth. Add this to the other pan and cook for 20 minutes. Add the mushrooms and monkfish. Season, cover and cook over a gentle heat for a further 25 minutes. Remove the bouquet garni and serve garnished with the croutons or *fleurons* if you are using them.

Further inland, in rugby-playing country, the cooking medium is white rather than red wine, laced, of course, with a little Armagnac.

La Lotte à la Gasconne

Monkfish as cooked in Gascony

2 monkfish tails, each weighing 450 g on the bone, 350 g filletted
2 tbsp seasoned flour
50 g butter
2 tbsp sunflower oil
100 g button mushrooms, halved or quartered according to size
1 large clove garlic, chopped
1 tbsp tomato purée
120 ml medium dry white wine
½ tbsp Armagnac
salt and pepper
1 tbsp chopped parsley

Skin and fillet the fish if not already done. Cut it into 5cm pieces and toss in the seasoned flour.

Heat the butter and oil in a frying pan over a good flame then put in the fish, mushrooms and garlic. Turn the fish to sear it on all sides, then add the tomato purée, wine and Armagnac. Reduce the heat and stir gently to blend the sauce, seasoning to taste.

Leave to cook slowly for a further 5 minutes not too long or the fish will become leathery.

Sprinkle with chopped parsley and serve with plain boiled rice.

The *département* of Roussillon is the southernmost in the country, having been ceded to France by Spain in 1694. Except in a few isolated areas, the inhabitants, though loyal Frenchmen, are proud of their Catalan inheritance, so their cooking is markedly influenced by Spanish style and ingredients. This is their distinctive way of serving *lotte,* as you might find it by the Mediterranean in Collioure.

La Lotte Catalane

Monkfish Catalan style

2 monkfish tails, skinned and boned, together weighing 700 g
3 sweet red peppers, deseeded and chopped
2 shallots, chopped
1 small orange, peeled and cut into small pieces
olive oil
2 tbsp capers
4 tbsp flaked almonds
salt and pepper
200 ml fairly sweet white wine
chopped parsley

Skin the fish and bone it if not already done. Cut the flesh into cubes. In a *sauteuse* (sauté pan) with a lid, soften the red peppers, shallots and orange in a little olive oil. Add the fish, the capers and almonds and season. After 1-2 minutes, add the wine and simmer until the fish is cooked, about 10 minutes. Do not overcook it. Sprinkle the parsley over when serving.

One of the specialities of Toulouse is their *aillade*, a walnut and garlic-based mixture with something of the texture of a mayonnaise. As well as finding it served as an accompaniment to duck, especially *magrets*, it makes a lively companion with *lotte*, the fish itself hardly needing an elaborate preparation in the face of such a strong sauce.

La Lotte Toulousaine

Monkfish served with walnut and garlic sauce

2 monkfish tails, boned and skinned
seasoned flour
3 tbsp olive oil
4 shallots, chopped
2 cloves garlic, chopped
150 ml *fumet de poisson* (fish stock)
salt and pepper

For the aillade toulousaine:
75 g shelled walnuts
50 g chopped garlic
salt and pepper
150 ml walnut oil
1 tbsp chopped parsley

First make the *aillade* by crushing the walnuts and garlic to a paste, or blend to as smooth a texture as possible in a mixer, seasoning and stirring in a dash of water if necessary. Work in the walnut oil little by little, finally adding the chopped parsley. The mayonnaise-like texture will soon become apparent.

To cook the fish, cut it into cubes and toss them in seasoned flour. Heat the oil in a *sauteuse* (sauté pan) and fry the pieces together with the shallots and garlic. Add the fish stock, stir well and then add the *aillade*. Check the seasoning.

Serve with saffron rice (turmeric can be substituted).

LES VIANDES

BEEF AND VEAL

FRANCE PRODUCES SOME OF THE best beef you can find. The country pastures of the Aubrac on the Aveyron/Cantal/Lozère borders are famous for the quality of their meat produce. The flavour is splendid, but it can be very tough; for English tastes it is not hung enough. Our local Aveyron butcher boasts that his is hung for at least 15 days, but it can still be heavy going. It seems that the longer you hang it (sometimes 45 days in the UK) the more tender it becomes, but it is then inclined to lose its flavour. The best answer in France lies perhaps in preferring long, slow-cooked stews.

Beef cheeks have become fashionable, even though they can be tough. However, if you can manage to find them from younger beasts they can be delicious. Long slow cooking at minimal temperatures is the secret.

Les Joues de Boeuf Aux Cèpes

Beef cheeks with mushrooms

300 g white haricot beans (Tarbais for preference, either fresh or soaked overnight if dried)
800 g beef cheeks, trimmed of excess fat
2 tbsp butter and oil
50 ml Armagnac
4 slices orange
4 cloves garlic
½ bottle good red wine
250 g fresh cèpes (100 g if dried) cut into bite-size pieces
salt and pepper

Boil the haricots for 45 minutes and drain all but 4 tbsp of the cooking water. Do not salt them.

Find a pan with a lid into which the cheeks will fit as snugly as possible, all in one piece or two if necessary. Do not cut into smaller pieces.

Heat the butter and oil in a pan, add the cheeks and sear all over at a good heat without browning them too much. Add the Armagnac and set alight. When the flames have died down, add the orange and garlic and pour the wine over. The liquid should come at least half-way up the meat, so if necessary, add a little water or beef stock (if you have any handy).

Cover and simmer as gently as possible so that the mixture barely bubbles. Cook for 2½ hours, then add the beans with the reserved cooking water if needed to give the sauce the desired consistency. Add the cèpes and continue cooking for a further 45 minutes.

A fresh green salad is all you will need as accompaniment.

o

At the end of the last century, the production of calves' meat suffered an eclipse, both in Britain and in France; in Britain largely because of the perceived cruelty in the raising and transport of the animals, and in France because of the ban placed by Italy on the importation of veal. There was also the collapse of the Italian economy, the outbreak of mad cow disease and the prejudice of the EU against meat production in favour of cereals. Veal suddenly became unmarketable, except for the liver and the shins for making *osso buco*. What happened (and is still happening in the UK) to the rest of the animal is a mystery. Even the once ever-popular escalopes have largely disappeared from all but a few British butcher shops.

In France, however, disaster was turned into rebirth. Gone is the white veal meat produced from animals raised on reconstituted milk. Groups of enthusiastic farmers have turned to the older methods of raising calves *sous la mère,* adding to the mother's milk cereal supplements deriving from genetically unmodified crops. Only the best breeds of cattle are used in this production and the result is a pink meat just like the veal that producers raised a hundred years ago. Close to our home we are lucky to have *Veau de l'Aveyron et du Ségala*, a recognised *appellation* for this kind of meat, covering an area from Castres in the south nearly to Aurillac in the north, and from Millau in the east almost to Rocamadour in the Lot.

Not surprisingly, this renaissance has given rise to the revival and in many cases the creation of interesting recipes for preparing veal. Shin of veal, as elsewhere, can be made into a kind of *osso buco*, but be sure the shin is from the back legs and not the front, where the flesh is much tougher. Here are a few suggestions that avoid the fancy practices of starred chefs and can be achieved at home.

There are other groups of growers all over the South-West, including in the Basque country where the traditional *axoa fricassée* is a local favourite.

L'Axoa de Veau Espelette

Veal with peppers and spices

4 tbsp sunflower oil
800 g shoulder of veal cut into bite-sized cubes
1 onion, finely chopped
1 tsp *piment d'Espelette* or 2 whole *piments*, deseeded and chopped fine
1 sweet red pepper
10 baby sweet green peppers cut in finger-sized strips
1 clove garlic
salt

Heat the oil in a large heavy-based pan. Fry all the ingredients, stirring, for 8 minutes over good heat, then for another 8 over reduced heat.

Cover and simmer another 10 minutes. The meat juices should clarify. Serve with *pommes rissolées.*

Le Puy, strictly part of the Auvergne, is one of the strangest of religious sites in France, with its famous cathedral perched on top of an extinct volcano, and known all over the world, especially to pilgrims on the way from Burgundy to Saint-Jacques-de Compostelle. It is also the heart of the production of the highly prized green lentils *du Puy,* which nowadays enjoy *label rouge* protection. In one of the enterprising restaurants in this touristy town, we found the lentils accompanying calves' liver in an interesting and new way. Served together, the natural sauce produced by the lentils blends beautifully with that from the liver.

La Foie de Veau au Miel et Citron Vert Avec les Lentilles du Puy

Calves' liver with lentils, lime and honey

4 tbsp duck or goose fat
1-2 shallots according to size, finely chopped
300 g lentilles du Puy
500 ml chicken stock (1 cube dissolved in water can be substituted)
650 g calves' liver, divided into 4 fairly thick pieces
1 tbsp juice of fresh lime
1 tbsp honey
salt and pepper

Heat half the fat in a heavy-based pan with a lid, then soften the shallots. Add the lentils and turn them in the fat before adding the stock, which should always cover the lentils. Cover and cook for about 1 hour fairly gently, adding more stock or water if necessary.

In a frying pan, sauté the liver in the remaining fat over a good fire. Cook for 1-2 minutes each side according to thickness; not more. It should remain pink in the centre. Remove to a warm place. Add the lime juice to the pan, scraping up any bits from the base, then add the honey and blend to make a fairly thin sauce.

Often it is the more modest parts of the calf that supply the most interesting dishes. This is because, in times gone by, the more expensive cuts were beyond the reach of country cooks. In a remote restaurant above the valley of the river Viaur, we were delighted to be served this version of a slowly cooked calf's heart, which Monique, the patronne, assured us is even better allowed to cool overnight and served reheated the following day. Alas, fashions change; Monique, who was much admired by a faithful band of fans, has retired and the restaurant has vanished with this recipe, but the memory remains.

Le Coeur de Veau au Madère

Veal heart cooked in wine and Madeira

1 veal heart, about 900 g
2 tbsp duck or goose fat or vegetable oil
300 g onions, sliced
bouquet garni
200 ml dry white wine
200 ml meat stock
1 tbsp cornflour or Maizena
2 tbsp Madeira
salt and pepper

Wash the heart and trim off any fat. Heat the fat in a large casserole and brown the heart all over. Remove and set aside. Add the onions to the pan and fry to a good colour. Put back the heart, add the *bouquet garni* and the wine and turn down the heat.

In a small pan, heat the meat stock then stir in the cornflour, diluted in a little cold water. Bring to the boil gently and, when it has thickened, add the contents to the casserole together with the Madeira; season.

Cover and leave on a very low heat to braise for 2 hours, turning the heart in the sauce halfway through. To serve, cut into slices, accompanied by the onions and the sauce.

Veal cheeks can be just as tasty as those of their parents but, being younger and less full-blooded, they do not require such a robust preparation. The wine is white, not red, and it would be wrong to offer a youngster Armagnac. *Joues de veau* are difficult to find commercially but you may be lucky at your local butcher, or he may be able to order them for you. Another possible source is the local country market, where a farmer-producer may have some already packed for sale.

Les Joues de Veau Braisées

Veal cheeks cooked in wine with herbs

880 g veal cheeks
generous sprigs of herbs: tarragon, savory, lovage, oregano, parsley, thyme, etc
half a bottle of dry white wine
4 cloves garlic, sliced
2 chicken stock cubes, crumbled
½ tsp piment d'Espelette
salt and pepper

Choose a *cocotte* with a tight-fitting lid into which the cheeks will just fit. Add the cheeks, then tuck the herbs all around, stuffing them to the bottom of the dish. Add the other ingredients and, if necessary a little water so that the veal is almost covered.

Bring slowly to the boil and simmer very gently for 3 hours.

Remove the meat and keep aside. Strain the contents of the pan, reserving the clear juice and adding it back into the pan with the veal, discarding the herbs. Simmer slowly together for another 30 minutes. Check for seasoning and serve with peas and new potatoes, either steamed or roasted.

If you ask at the butcher for some veal with which to make a *blanquette*, he will often propose the part of the animal called *collier*. It has the advantage of being largely lean so needs little trimming. As well as being suitable for *blanquettes* the *collier* can also be used for a variety of braised dishes that bring out the flavour of the meat just as successfully. From a variety of preparations, here is our composite version, especially recommended in late summer when the *haricots Tarbais* can be bought fresh or in the pod.

Le Collier de Veau Aux Haricots Tarbais

Neck of veal with white beans

700 g unpodded fresh *haricots Tarbais* (half the weight after podding or if using soaked dried beans)
3 tbsp duck or goose fat
1 large onion, cut in rings
250 g *lardons* (or green (unsmoked) streaky bacon diced into cubes)
250 g chestnut mushrooms, cut into chunky pieces
800 g *collier* (neck) of veal, boned and cut into generous-sized pieces
1½ tbsp flour
1 tsp piment d'Espelette
salt and pepper
200 ml dry white wine
1 chicken stock cube, crumbled

Pod the beans and boil gently in unseasoned water for 1 hour.

Meanwhile, in a *cocotte* with a tight-fitting lid, heat the fat then briefly soften the onion, *lardons* and mushrooms in the fat over a low fire for 5 minutes without browning them. Add the veal, raising the heat slightly and browning the meat on all sides.

Add the flour and seasoning and mix well. Continue cooking for 5-10 minutes. Add the wine and chicken stock cube and water barely to cover. Bring all to the boil, cover and simmer gently for 1 hour. Add the cooked beans to the pot and continue simmering for another 15 minutes.

Serve with a salad. If preferred, potatoes may be used instead of the beans. Not the same, though.

———o———

If you explore the supermarkets in the South-West, you will probably find the shelves of already-packed meats devoted almost exclusively to pork in its various guises. The reason is not hard to find; in former times pork was virtually the only meat available to peasant-proprietors, who reared their own pig but only rarely pastured cattle or sheep. Today the custom lingers, and pork features very largely in the local cuisine. It goes to make the sausages (both in their traditional country version as well as the more sophisticated Toulouse kind); *boudins*, the local style in blood puddings; the *lardons* which are so useful in the preparation of slow-cooked braises, as well as the moistening of dried roasting birds such as guinea fowl; and it is the base of so many *pâtés* and terrines.

In its most festive preparation it is roasted, whether simply or with mushrooms or sometimes truffles, and usually served hot. It seems, however, that pork has a better flavour and indeed texture when cold, especially when prepared in the following version. This is an old recipe from the Périgord that preserves the natural moisture of the meat as well as its flavour.

Le Rôti Porc Froid Marie Robert

Cooked pork loin served cold

Make sure the butcher gives you the bones and rind, and think ahead because you will need three days to achieve the best result.

1 kg loin of pork, boned and rolled
2-3 cloves garlic, chopped into pieces for spiking the meat
1 onion stuck with 2 cloves
1 carrot, sliced
1 leek, sliced
bouquet garni
500 ml chicken stock
salt and pepper

Day One
Spike the meat with the garlic, season well, cover and refrigerate overnight.

Day Two
Put the meat with its rind and bones into a tight-fitting *cocotte* with the vegetables and the *bouquet garni*, cover with the stock and (if need be) additional cold water. Cover with the lid, bring to the boil and simmer slowly for 1 hour. Remove the lid and allow to continue cooking until the liquid has virtually evaporated, leaving the fat and the vegetables only with the meat (1 to 1½ hours 73pprox.). Let it all take on colour in the juices.

Remove the joint from the pot, sieve the pan juices over, and allow to cool for 24 hours, until covered with a jellied glaze…

Day Three
Serve with a salad.

Pork chops from the loin look so appetizing, the lean meat bordered by a thin layer of fat and often sold with the skin. Grilled, they can often be tough and rather boring, but try some chops from the shoulder, sold with the rind and the fat integrated into the flesh of the meat. Don't grill them either, but gently sautée, add some good stock and serve simply with potatoes and green vegetables.

If you prefer your pork hot and roasted more traditionally, this version works well, the meat enhanced by the accompanying seasoning and vegetables.

Le Porc Rôti en Cocotte

Roast pork

800 g loin of pork (or rolled shoulder)
2 cloves garlic
2 tsp thyme leaves
1 tbsp lemon juice
1 large onion, finely chopped
400 gr potatoes, chopped into 2cm cubes
salt and pepper

Season the pork, spike it with the garlic and thyme, squeeze lemon juice over and leave to stand for 1-2 hours.

Preheat the oven to 220C/450 F/gas mark 7. Place the joint in a *cocotte* with a tight-fitting lid and roast it uncovered for 25 minutes. Lower the heat to 160C/350F/gas mark 3 and add the onion and potatoes. Cover with the lid. After a further 25 minutes raise the temperature back to 220C/450F/gas mark 7 to brown the contents of the *cocotte.*

Celery, either braised in butter or puréed, makes a good accompaniment.

Just as the boning of a duck leaves behind on the carcass scraps of flesh which make wonderful *grattons*, so with the pig. When the legs are cut from the body there is left behind a quantity of small pieces of meat, which are some of the most tender and succulent of all. They are called *araignées.* You can buy them just as they are in their natural state, or marinated in herbs and spices. Here is how they are cooked quite simply. If you prefer them marinated, substitute the juices from the marinade and leave out the wine – at least until the last moment in case the pan needs deglazing.

Les Araignées de Porc

Pork scratchings

2 tbsp duck or goose fat
800 g araignées
2 cloves garlic, finely chopped
2 shallots, chopped
4 sprigs fresh thyme (1 heaped tsp dried)
125 ml dry white wine
50ml verjus, plus extra to deglaze (optional)
salt and pepper

Heat the fat in a heavy-based pan, then add the *araignées*, season and sear well. Add the garlic and shallot, the thyme, half of the wine, the verjus and simmer gently for 30 minutes. Deglaze the pan with the remaining wine or (better) with verjus if you have it.

While pork chops from the loin are universally popular, we find them dry and less tender than if cut from the shoulder (*échine).* Slowly braised, they retain all their flavour and juiciness.

Les Côtes de Porc Mijotés

Braised pork chops

4 pork chops from the shoulder (*échine*)
1 onion, sliced into rings
1 carrot, chopped
200 ml white wine
500 ml chicken stock
salt and pepper

Lay the chops in a *sauteuse* (sauté pan) with a tight-fitting lid. Spread the vegetables around, add the wine and stock. Season.

Bring to simmering point and allow to cook slowly for 40 minutes, turning the chops over halfway through the cooking.

Remove the chops and keep warm, then reduce the cooking juices until they form a slightly thickened sauce. Pour over the chops and the vegetables and serve with steamed potatoes.

In the Auvergne, it is not surprising that local cooks profit from the abundance of good cream from their cattle, and contrast it with the relative blandness of cabbage. The combination goes well with pork chops.

Les Côtes de Porc Á l'Auvergnate

Pork chops with cabbage and cream

1 medium-sized white cabbage, sliced finely
150 ml double cream
2 tbsp butter, plus extra to dot
120 ml white wine
4 sage leaves, finely chopped
4 pork chops (preferably from the *échine*)
6 tbsp grated Cantal cheese
salt and pepper

Boil the cabbage in salted water for 7 minutes. Drain, season, return to the pan, add the cream and simmer slowly for 30 minutes.

Preheat the oven to 160 C/320F/gas mark 4.

In another pan, heat the butter, add the chops and sauté until they are brown and well cooked through (about 20 minutes). Remove from the pan and season them. Stir the wine into the pan juices, add the sage and allow to bubble for a couple of minutes. Stir this juice into the creamed cabbage.

Spread half of the cabbage mixture on the bottom of a baking dish, lay the chops on top and cover with the rest of the cabbage. Sprinkle with the cheese and a few dots of butter and bake in the oven for 20 minutes until the top is golden brown.

In spring a pork fillet can be enjoyed as a trio, with the youngest new potatoes and fresh new asparagus as fitting partners.

Le Filet de Porc Printanier

Pork fillet with asparagus and new potatoes

30 g butter
12-16 button onions, peeled
800 g pork fillet, cut into 2cm cubes
1 tbsp flour
150 ml dry white wine
150 ml water
4 cloves garlic, coarsely chopped
300 g small new potatoes
24 small asparagus spears
100 ml prune juice (optional)
4 tbsp crème fraîche
salt and pepper

Melt the butter in *a sauteuse* (sauté pan) and soften the onions in it. Add the pieces of pork and cook them without browning. Stir in the flour, followed by the wine and water to make a sauce. Add the garlic, cover and simmer slowly for 45 minutes.

Meanwhile, steam the potatoes.

Add the prune juice to the pan (if using) with and asparagus, season and simmer for 15 minutes. Stir some of the sauce into the *crème fraîche* and return to the pan. Cook gently for 15 minutes without boiling. Check for seasoning, add the cooked potatoes and serve all together.

o

During the winter, the country people (and of course the wholesalers and butchers) will have put away joints of pork breast and salted them for future use. The degree of saltiness can vary, so the degree to which you will need to prepare the meat by prior soaking will depend accordingly. This is the traditional way of cooking them with lentils; simple but eternally popular.

Le Petit Salé Aux Lentilles

Pork belly with lentils

8 slices of pork belly (about 600g)
250 ml. chicken stock
1 large onion, cut into thin rings
2 medium-sized carrots, sliced
2 bay leaves
12 peppercorns
salt and pepper

For the lentils
2 tbsp duck or goose fat
1 shallot, finely chopped
300 g lentilles du Puy
150 ml chicken stock
2 tbsp butter
4 tsp ginger paste
2 tsp Dijon mustard

Choose a *cocotte* with a tight-fitting lid into which the pork will fit and arrange the meat in one layer. Pour over the chicken stock to barely cover, season, bring slowly to the boil and simmer for 45 minutes.

Meanwhile, prepare the lentils. Melt the goose or duck fat in a pan and sauté the shallot until soft but not browned. Add the lentils, season and mix with the fat. Cover with the chicken stock and cook over a medium heat for 40 minutes or so, adding more stock or water until the lentils will absorb no more, but are still moist. Check for seasoning.

Preheat the grill to high. Remove the pork from its liquor. Mix together the butter, ginger and mustard and spread over the surface of the pork pieces. Grill until nicely browned.

Serve the pork surrounded with the lentils. A few sautéed tomato halves add colour to a dish more admired for its taste than its appearance.

In the deep South-West, under the lee of the Pyrenees, the Catalans have a way of making spicy balls of meat in which they mix equal quantities of pork with beef, which is a trifle removed from what they do further north, but a tasty change, nonetheless.

Les Boles de Picolat

Meatballs with olives and mushrooms

400 g minced pork
400 g minced beef
2 eggs
2 cloves garlic, finely chopped
flour, for dusting
olive oil
1 onion, finely chopped
100 g *lardons*
50 g tomato concentrate
200 g green olives, stoned and chopped
150 g mushrooms (*cèpes* for choice) cut into bite-sized pieces
salt and pepper

In a bowl, mix the meats, eggs and garlic; season. Shape into balls the size of a large walnut and flour them. Heat some olive oil in a pan, add the meatballs and brown them all over.

In a *cocotte,* soften the onion and *lardons* in more oil. Stir in the tomato concentrate, a little flour and a glass of water. Simmer for 15 minutes. Add the meat balls, olives and mushrooms. Add water to cover and simmer gently for 45 minutes.

Simply boiled rice would perhaps be the best accompaniment.

There are conflicting traditions about the preparation of lamb for the table. In former times, the country-people considered it relatively lacking in taste (*fade*). The *bourgeoisie,* however, valued it highly, and the contrast is evident today in the fairly high price of the meat. Furthermore, sheep were primarily raised for their wool and, above all, their milk which was made into cheese and sent to Roquefort for maturing. Nowadays cheese from *brebis* (as the ewes are called) is made all over the South-West and the Basque people no longer make the trip to Roquefort but have a thriving industry of their own.

The lambing season in the South-West is relatively early, beginning at Christmastime and overlapping into the New Year. This means that the best time for enjoying lamb at the table is in the late summer and early autumn, before the sheep age and become more muttony.

Individual lamb chops, from whichever part of the animal, are simple enough to grill, but a *carré* may be better roasted.

Le Carré d'Agneau

Roasted lamb cutlets

8 medium-sized cloves garlic
2 *carrés* (6 or 7 cutlets) prepared in the French way by your butcher
best olive oil
6 tsp salt
pepper
1 tsp piment d'Espelette
4 tsp ground cumin
120 ml white wine
2 tbsp redcurrant jelly, plus extra to serve

Preheat the oven to 260C/500F/gas mark 7.

Cut the garlic into slivers and insert one in between each of the lamb bones. Cut a trench along the lean side of the cutlets where they adjoin the bones and insert more garlic pieces the length of the trench. Brush the *carré* on both sides with oil. Make a *sel épicé* with the seasonings and sprinkle lightly on both sides of the *carré*.

Put the lamb into a roasting tin with 2 tbsp of oil and any remaining cloves of garlic chopped finely. Roast the *carré* for 25 minutes, turning the oven down to 200C/400F/gas mark 6 after 15 minutes. Transfer the meat to a warm place to rest for a further 10 minutes.

While the meat is resting, pour the wine into the roasting tin and scrape up the juices with a wooden spoon. Add the redcurrant jelly and allow it to melt in the juices over a low simmer. Serve this sauce separately with more cold redcurrant jelly.

Sometimes it is difficult to find lamb's kidneys for sale in more than just one or two at a time. If you can find more, this is a quick and easy way of preparing them.

Les Rognons d'Agneau Aux Champignons

Lamb's kidneys with mushrooms

60 g unsalted butter
1 large shallot, finely chopped
200 g mushrooms, roughly sliced
6 lamb's kidneys, halved and cored
150 ml white wine
salt and pepper

Heat the butter in a heavy-based pan, add the shallot and mushrooms and cook gently, stirring, for 5 minutes.

Raise the heat a bit and, in the centre of the pan, sear the open side of the kidneys. Turn them, season and allow to simmer slowly for 8 minutes.

Raise the heat further and add the wine, allowing it to bubble away until you have a short sauce. Check for seasoning and serve hot with rice or *pommes purées* (mashed potato).

While local people tend generally to serve their lamb pink, or even rare, a shoulder requires longer cooking to release the larger proportion of fat. For this reason it is sometimes served after long cooking, rather than as a quick roast.

l'Agneau Braisé aux Légumes

Lamb shoulder braised with vegetables

1 tbsp duck or goose fat
1 medium-sized onion } all roughly chopped
1 large carrot } all roughly chopped
1 stick celery } all roughly chopped
4 cloves garlic } all roughly chopped
600 g shoulder of lamb, cut into 3cm cubes
1 vegetable stock cube
1 glass white wine
1 tsp piment d'Espelette
300 g ratte potatoes
salt and pepper

Heat the fat in a *cocotte* with a tight-fitting lid, then sweat the chopped vegetables without browning them. Add the lamb pieces. Dissolve the stock cube in a little water and add to the *cocotte* with the wine. Pour over water to cover, season, bring to the boil and allow to simmer very gently for 2 hours.

Meanwhile, partly boil the potatoes for 15 minutes. Add the potatoes to the *cocotte* for the second hour of the cooking. Serve from the pot.

o

Lamb shanks have become more and more popular over the years, and their price once minimal, has been rising accordingly. They need long slow cooking, so start the day before if you can. If your butcher knows their origin, he will be able to tell you whether they come from the front or the rear end of the sheep. Those from the back of the sheep are the more tender.

Les Souris d'Agneau en Casserole

Casserole of lamb shanks

5 tbsp duck or goose fat
1 large onion (all thinly sliced)
2 large carrots (all thinly sliced)
2 outer sticks of celery (all thinly sliced)
1 large leek (all thinly sliced)
4 lamb shanks
3 tbsp flour
½ bottle white wine
1 tsp piment d'Espelette
1½ tsp ground cumin
2 bay leaves
salt and a little freshly ground pepper

Preheat the oven to 160C/350F/gas mark 4.

In a lidded casserole big enough to hold the shanks in one layer, heat 2 tbsp of the fat, then soften the vegetables very gently, without colouring them.

In another wide pan, brown the shanks well in the remaining fat. Remove and put aside. Stir the flour into the remaining fat and make a *roux* in the usual way. Gradually add the wine and enough water to make a fairly runny sauce. Simmer together for 5 minutes.

In the casserole, bury the shanks among the vegetables and pour the sauce over them. Add water if necessary, so that the liquid nearly covers the meat. Add the cumin and the bay leaves and season. Allow to boil, covered, over a medium heat for a few minutes. Transfer to the oven; after 10 minutes, reduce the heat to 105C/220F/gas mark 1). Cook for 2 hours. Remove from the oven and cool overnight to allow the fat to come to the top.

Next day, skim the fat from the surface as best you can (the meat and the vegetables will get in your way). Top up with water to cover if necessary. Heat the oven to 160C/375F/gas mark 4. Bring the casserole to a boil on top of the stove then transfer to the oven. Reduce the heat as on the previous day and cook for another 2 hours. Taste for seasoning.

Potatoes in their jackets (*robes de champ*) will enjoy the sauce. Failing their availability (difficult to find large enough baking potatoes in France) steamed potatoes can substitute. A green vegetable will add colour to the plate.

o

There is something celebratory about a leg of lamb, however it is prepared, whether simply roasted, slow-cooked for 7 hours, or baked with anchovies as in Gascony. Its affinity with garlic is undisputed, and it is difficult to think of a *gigot* prepared without it. Try this eccentric version, another recipe from M. Bardou at Lautrec, where the best garlic comes from. You can reduce the amount of garlic if you like, but M. Bardou would probably not approve.

Le Gigot d'Agneau à la Crème d'Ail Rose de Lautrec

Roast leg of lamb with pink Lautrec garlic sauce

Serves 6

2 tbsp olive oil
1 *gigot* weighing about 1.5kg
3 whole heads of Lautrec garlic
500 ml whole milk
cornflour, Maizena or similar (optional)
salt and pepper

Brush the oil all over the *gigot*, season and roast at 200C/375F/gas mark 6 for 1¼ hours.

While it is cooking, prepare the sauce. Peel the garlic and put it in a saucepan with the milk, season and allow to simmer until the garlic is melting. Crush it well with a fork.

When the *gigot* is done, pour the pan juices into the sauce, thickening it with a liaison of cornflour if it is not thick enough for your taste. Serve carved *gigot* with the sauce.

o

The increase of immigration, particularly of students studying at universities such as Toulouse and Montpellier, has led to the introduction of Moroccan elements into local cooking. We particularly like this gentle *tagine,* which you can make easily without the pretty traditional-shaped pot with a conical lid used in Morocco.

La Tagine d'Agneau Aux Abricots

Tagine of lamb with apricots

250 g dried apricots
750 g shoulder of lamb, cut into 3cm cubes
1 onion, cut into rings
1 vegetable stock cube, crumbled
2 tsp ground cumin
2 tsp ras-el-hanout
½ cinnamon stick
2 tsp cardamom seeds
¼ lemon
2 sprigs mint
750 ml water
100 g flaked almonds
2 tsp butter
salt and pepper

Put the apricots in a heatproof bowl, pour over boiling water to cover and leave them to soak for 40 minutes.

Meanwhile, put all the remaining ingredients, except the almonds, into a casserole with a tight-fitting lid. They should be just about covered with the 750 ml water. Bring to the boil and simmer gently for 1 hour.

A few minutes before serving, brown the almonds in the butter and add to the casserole. Serve with couscous.

o

Blanquette de veau is often named as one of France's most-loved dishes, but a blanquette made from lamb is less well-known and well worth sampling.

La Blanquette d'Agneau

Blanquette of lamb

Serves 2-4

half a shoulder of lamb (for 2)
  or half a leg of lamb (for 4)
1 tbsp duck or goose fat
1 large onion, sliced
bouquet garni
1 bouillon cube, crumbled
40g button mushrooms
salt and pepper

For the sauce
30g butter
1 tbsp flour
1 egg yolk
1 tbsp lemon juice
grated nutmeg

Bone the lamb and remove the fat. Cut it into 3cm cubes. Melt the duck fat in a lidded casserole and brown the meat in batches. Add the onion, the *bouquet garni* and the bouillon cube, then pour in enough hot water to cover the contents. Cover the casserole and leave to simmer gently for 1 hour, then add the mushrooms and continue the cooking for a further 30 minutes.

For the sauce, in a small pan melt the butter, stir in the flour and just enough stock from the meat to make a sauce. Beat together the egg yolk and lemon juice and add it to the sauce, then pour the sauce back over the meat. Check the seasoning, adding a little grated nutmeg and serve.

o

Just as Madame Issaly at Domaine de Ramaye in Gaillac has given us the ultimate in *Coq au vin*, her slow-cooked lamb stew must be the best there is: rich and flavoursome. You will need to start two days ahead of time, so this is hardly fast food. So much the better.

La Daube de Mouton Issaly

Madame Issaly's lamb stew

110 g salt belly of pork, cut into cubes
A good piece of pork rind (optional)
I pig's trotter split in half (optional)
1 kg boned shoulder of lamb, cut into chunks
1 onion, chopped
2 carrots, chopped
2 tomatoes, skinned and chopped
3 large cloves garlic, chopped
½ bottle red wine (Domaine de Ramaye, of course)
2 tbsp walnut oil
bouquet garni
25 g flour
pinch of quatre-épices
salt and pepper

Day One
Put the belly of pork in a large pan of cold water with the rind and the trotter. Bring slowly to the boil and cook gently for 30 minutes. Drain and discard the water.

Put them in a large shallow dish with the lamb and all the other ingredients. Stir to combine well and leave to marinate in a cool place for at least 6 hours.

Preheat the oven to 180C/350F/gas mark 4.

Choose your cooking pot carefully. Either it must have a concave lid which you can fill with water, or you will need an enamel plate which fits tightly, and which you can fill with water and use instead of a lid.

Push all the ingredients down into the pot so that they are covered by the liquid and season. Bring slowly to the boil on top of the stove, then put the casserole in the oven with its lid, which you fill with cold water. After 10 minutes reduce the temperature to as low as it will go (105C/220 F/gas mark ¼). Cook for 3 hours, topping up the liquid in the lid from time to time. Remove from the oven and leave to cool.

Day Two

Remove as much fat as possible from the casserole and discard the pork and trotter. Preheat the oven to 180C/350F/gas mark 4 and reheat the casserole, filling the concave lid with water as before, for 10-15 minutes. Reduce to the lowest possible temperature and cook for another 3 hours, watching the water level in the lid.

LES LÉGUMES

VEGETABLES HAVE ALWAYS BEEN THE backbone of diet in the South-West, more important than meat even, because they could always be picked from the *potager*. Eaten on their own, or used as a flavouring for other foods, they are never absent from the menu. For the gardener, the season does not begin in the spring but in the previous autumn with the planting of seeds and plants to produce the young vegetables for the following year: peas, broad beans and potatoes, for example. Those with an asparagus bed will need to tend it during the winter. Spring will see the sowing of tomato seeds or, when the danger of frost has gone by, young plants. Green beans and lettuces will be sown in succession to provide a never-ceasing supply of these favourite vegetables throughout the summer, while marrows and pumpkins in all their variety will follow soon after. Cabbage is left in the ground over the winter (some are biennial) so that they develop the flowering sprouts that are highly prized the following spring. Nature also provides its own vegetable for the table: the wild *tamier (Tamus communis)*, called black bryony in English but *respontchous* (in various spellings) in the South-West of France. The shoots must be cooked, and not eaten raw, and the berries are not to be eaten.

Growing vegetables to supply supermarkets has developed into a huge industry, much of the produce being produced intensively and artificially. It tends to have much less flavour and character than that produced in the *potager*, and its shelf-life is often short. So, if you don't grow your own, buy locally at the market or from local sources.

Potatoes became the staple food of the Aveyron, succeeding the chestnut when the railways were able to bring lime to an otherwise impoverished soil. They remain an essential feature of so many soups throughout the South-West, and few meals are served without potatoes in one form or another. They come in many varieties, from the very floury to the quite hard, so you need to ask the supplier which kind he is offering and its texture, or alternatively specify the kind you know what you want them for.

Pommes frites are a national favourite and need no commendation or guidance in their cooking. *Pommes rissolées* are another matter and need careful attention. These are small cubes of potato, fried in duck or goose fat so that that inside remains soft but the outside are crisp and golden. Ideal with grilled meats.

Les Pommes de Terre Rissolées

Cubed potatoes fried in goose fat

Serves 2

Choose all-purpose potatoes, neither too floury nor too firm. You will need a large pan (preferably non-stick) if you are to serve more than 2, because the potatoes need to cook in one layer.

300 g potatoes, peeled and cut into 1cm cubes
2 tbsp duck or goose fat
persillade (chopped parsley and 2 cloves of garlic, finely chopped)
salt and pepper

Steam the cubed potatoes for 10 minutes while you melt the fat over a low flame in a solid frying pan (preferably non-stick). Drain the potatoes and allow them to dry.

Transfer to the pan and turn them so that they are evenly coated in the fat. Season.

Cook slowly for 20 minutes, turning them from time to time, then raise the heat and cook, turning as needed, until they are nicely browned all over.

Just before serving add the *persillade,* mix well and cook together for 3 minutes.

We happen to have a neighbour who is one of the best cooks we know. In a country that boasts of its saffron revival, she has evolved this delicious way of marrying it with potatoes.

Les Petits Pommes de Terre au Safran

Saffron scented little potatoes

30 g clarified butter
600 g small waxy potatoes (rattes would be ideal) of the same size, peeled
2 good pinches of saffron threads
1 bay leaf
1 tsp thyme leaves, stripped from their stalk
150 ml chicken stock
1 tsp salt

Rehydrate the saffron threads in 2 tbsp hot water for 15 minutes.

Melt the butter in a lidded saucepan over a medium heat. Add the potatoes, cover with the lid and cook gently for 5 minutes. Add the saffron and its liquor, bay leaf and thyme and shake the pan to distribute the flavourings over the potatoes. Add the stock and some salt, cover and cook over a medium heat for 15-20 minutes, shaking the pan occasionally.

Remove the lid, bring to a fast boil and cook until the stock has evaporated and the potatoes are tender beautifully glazed and shiny with the saffron butter.

Another near neighbour of ours has, like so many other French people, another house, this time in the Ardèche, where this next recipe may originate. Lovely with game or roast meats.

Les Pommes de Terre Michèle Gaune

Potatoes with mustard and herbs

4 all-purpose potatoes
generously sized (1 each)
1 tbsp Dijon mustard
2 tbsp olive oil
herbes de Provence
salt and pepper

Peel the potatoes and steam them for 10 minutes.

Preheat the oven to 150C/300F/gas mark 2.

In a bowl mix together the mustard, oil, herbs and seasoning. Coat the potatoes in this mixture and put them to finish cooking in the oven for 30-45 minutes.

o

During our travels we came across a delightful way of roasting smallish potatoes in their skins. Back home in the Aveyron, we have tried to replicate this, and this is the nearest we can get to what we tasted with such enjoyment many years ago.

Les Pommes de Terre Orbec

Roast potatoes in their skins

4 tbsp duck or goose fat
6 medium-floury potatoes, the size of a duck's egg, unpeeled
salt and pepper

Preheat the oven to 200C/400 F/gas mark 6.

In a roasting tin, melt the fat on top of the stove without letting it get too hot.

Cut each potato in half lengthwise and lay cut surface downwards in the pan. Keep the heat low so that the potatoes do not stick but that their cut surfaces became slightly hard and crispy.

Turn the potatoes cut-surface uppermost. Season and transfer to the oven. Roast for 25 minutes.

Turn the potatoes so that their cut surface is downwards in the fat and roast for a further 25 minutes, but don't let the open sides burn. The skins should by this time have shrivelled and the face of the potatoes developed an attractive roasted colour.

Serve with grilled or roasted meats.

Potatoes are also capable of being elevated gastronomically when allied to the truffle. Maybe it was in the Lot at Lalbenque, world epicentre of the so-called black diamond, that Gilles Marre, the famous chef from Le Balandre at Cahors, got this idea for a delicious potato salad.

La Salade de Pommes de Terre Aux Truffes

Potato and truffle salad

50 g truffles, brushed clean and rinsed in running water
3 tbsp sunflower oil
1 tbsp best olive oil
450 waxy potatoes (e.g. Charlotte or Roseval)
1 tbsp verjuice or mild white wine vinegar
salt and pepper

Slice the truffles as thinly as possible, place in a bowl with the two oils and marinate for 2 hours at least.

Meanwhile, boil or steam the potatoes in their skins until they can be pierced with a skewer. Peel and then slice them.

Drain the truffles and make a dressing with the oils and the verjuice. It should be quite mild. Season with salt and pepper.

Toss the potatoes in the dressing while they are still warm, sprinkle the sliced truffle on top and serve.

One of the first delights of spring is the appearance of *reponchous*, spelt in various ways, the local name for *tamier (Tamus communis)* or black bryony. At first sight it looks like a kind of wild asparagus but has no affinity whatever. It is a climbing plant, weaving its long stems up the trees in the woods of the Aveyron and the Tarn in particular, where it is regarded as part of the *patrimoine* on a level with the *cassoulet*. It needs only brief cooking to prevent it developing an increasingly bitter flavour. Although it is for some people a cultivated taste, it is as much prized by country people in spring as *cèpes* are in autumn: they are both free gifts of nature. Try it blanched for a minute or two and serve with scrambled eggs and a little tarragon and/or chives; or more elaborately with some *lardons*, potatoes, garlic and parsley; or simply with a *vinaigrette* and chopped hard-boiled eggs.

Sometimes *reponchous* is called *l'asperge du pauvre*, but nowadays even the less fortunate cultivate real asparagus in their *potager*. Arguments will rage over whether the green or white kind is the better, the basic difference being in their cultivation– the white being virtually subterranean and thus deprived of the sunlight which might turn it mauve or green. Recipes for the two kinds seem interchangeable and extend far beyond the delicious way of serving it simply with melted butter and salt. Fashion has it that the fatter the stems the better and the more expensive to buy, but thinner stems can be equally delicious, as we discovered when we stayed at a remote country *auberge* near Bordeaux and the proprietor served us and gave us this recipe.

Le Ragoût d'Asperges

Asparagus stew

- 32 thin green asparagus spears
- 500 ml chicken stock
- 2 tbsp duck or goose fat
- 1 large onion, finely chopped
- 150 g salt belly of pork (or thickly cut green (unsmoked) bacon), cut into dice
- 2 tbsp flour
- salt, pepper and grated nutmeg

Clean and scrape the asparagus, setting aside the stems. Heat the stock in a shallow pan and simmer the asparagus in the stock for 30 minutes. Strain and reserve the stock.

In a large *sauteuse*, heat the fat, then add the onion and cook over a gentle heat to soften. Add the pork and continue for 15 minutes. Add the flour, mix well then add the reserved stock, little by little, to make a sauce. Allow all to simmer together for a further 10 minutes. Poach the asparagus in the sauce until just cooked but still quite firm; it should be tender but not soggy. Season with salt, pepper and grated nutmeg then serve, either as a dish on its own or as an accompaniment to plainly roasted poultry.

o

Other vegetables can be prepared in a similar way, and in early summer the following *ragoût* can be made from the deliciously young vegetables, especially if grown at home or acquired fresh from the market (stale versions from supermarkets will not do at all, or at least not as well).

Le Ragoût de Petits Légumes Printaniers

Mixed spring vegetables

- 350 g young broad beans, weighed in the pod
- 175 g *petits pois*, weighed in the pod
- 175 g *haricots verts (*French beans)
- 60 g duck or goose fat or butter
- 100 g raw country ham, cut in one slice, then diced
- 125 g young carrots, sliced into rings
- 8 button onions, peeled
- 1 tbsp flour
- 300 ml chicken stock
- 300 g tiny new potatoes, scrubbed
- *sarriette* (savory), finely chopped
- salt and pepper

Pod the broad beans (removing the inner skin unless they are tiny) and the peas. Top and tail the *haricots verts*.

Melt the fat in a large saucepan, add the ham, carrots and onions and cook very gently in the fat, softening the vegetables over low heat for 10 minutes, so that they do not take on colour. Stir occasionally.

Add the flour. Mix all well and add the stock little by little. Allow all to cook slowly for 5 minutes. Add the potatoes, cover the pan and boil gently for 20 minutes. Season, but be careful with the salt because of the ham. Add the *sarriette*, then the peas, broad beans and *haricots verts* and cook all together for another 7 minutes. The potatoes and onions should be well cooked but the green vegetables slightly *craquants*.

Whatever salad vegetables may be in season can be the basis of this simple salad topped with a fried egg.

La Salade Campagnarde

Salad of vegetables, eggs and ham in walnut oil dressing

2 tbsp duck or goose fat
400 g raw country ham or salt belly of pork, cut in thick slices
salad vegetables as available
walnut oil dressing
4 eggs, one per person
freshly ground pepper

Melt the fat in a pan, add the ham or pork and fry very gently in the fat while you prepare and dress the salad and arrange it on each person's plate.

Put the meat on top of each salad, and, in the remaining fat, fry the eggs with which you top the salad. Season with pepper; you will not need salt.

Salads can be quite elaborate. At a formal dinner to celebrate the annual Marcillac wine festival, they have been known to serve this elaborate dish featuring meats and various fruits, here reduced to proportions for 4 people.

La Salade Vigneronne

Salad of mixed meats, fruits and nuts

green salad, dressed with a *vinaigrette* lightly seasoned with a little curry powder
12 slices of smoked *magret de canard*
250 g *tête de veau* , bought pre-cooked and cut into small cubes
black grapes from Marcillac
1 orange, divided into segments
12 walnuts, shelled and kept in quarters

Serve the salad on to each person's plate, decorated and dressed with the other ingredients.

o

The French do not allow broad beans to assume the monstrous proportions more familiar to Anglo-Saxons. When the pods are little larger than pea-pods, they can be eaten whole, unpeeled and gently steamed. Or they can be podded and eaten raw as an *amuse-gueule* with salt. While still young, they are best cooked simply as in the following recipe .

Les Fèves en Sauce

Broad beans in a cream sauce

1 kg broad beans
30 g butter
2 tbsp crème fraîche
parsley, chives, marjoram, and other herbs to taste
salt and pepper

Shell and peel the broad beans, removing the inner skins. Steam them for 8 minutes, drain and turn into a pan with the melted butter. Stir in the cream and add the finely chopped herbs. Season to taste.

The expansion of the vegetable repertoire in the South-West is best illustrated by the adoption of the aubergine, a taste imported largely from Provence and the Languedoc, and it has given rise to a host of recipes (the best known of which are *ratatouille* and *pipérade*) with which to present them, either on their own or, more usually, in combination with tomatoes. It is not surprising that aubergine also features in Spanish cooking, reflecting perhaps the common Mediterranean culture imported from Roman days. *Escalivada* is a roasted vegetable dish is typical of the Roussillon. Its name comes from a verb in Catalan meaning to roast in the embers.

A country dish, it is made from roasted tomatoes, aubergines, peppers and onions. Typically served warm or at room temperature with crusty bread, or to accompany meat or fish in warmer months, it is suitable to eat all year round. Best prepared and eaten the same day.

Escalivada de Légumes (Catalan)

Roasted vegetables

2 medium-sized aubergines (about 900 g)
extra virgin olive oil2 red bell peppers
2 medium-sized onions, peeled
1 head garlic
4 firm tomatoes
1 or 2 2-oz cans anchovy fillets
salt

Preheat the oven to 180C/350F/gas mark 4.

Line a large roasting pan with aluminum foil. (If a large pan is not available, use two smaller pans.)

Cut the aubergines in half lengthwise, brush the cut side with olive oil and place cut-side down in the tin. Make small slits in the skin so that they don't split open as they cook.

Place the peppers, onions and head of garlic in the tin. Brush all vegetables with olive oil and sprinkle with salt. Roast in the oven for about 1 hour, turning the vegetables over after 30 minutes or so.

After 1 hour, add the tomatoes to the pan and continue roasting until all the vegetables are cooked, for another 20-30 minutes. If the peppers are thoroughly cooked while others need more time, remove them from the pan and continue roasting the rest.

Remove from the oven and allow to cool. Carefully remove the skin from the peppers and aubergines. Cut the roasted vegetables into strips and place them on a platter or tray with the anchovy fillets. Sprinkle with a little salt and drizzle with extra virgin olive oil.

Escalivada is typically served at room temperature with plenty of sliced bread.

The same family of ingredients can be used in quite a different way to make a savoury *gratin.*

La Bohémienne

Vegetable gratin

1 medium-sized aubergine (about 450 g)
olive oil
350 g tomatoes, peeled, quartered and de-seeded
1 large clove garlic, chopped
2 anchovy fillets
2 tbsp flour
2 tbsp milk
fresh breadcrumbs
salt and pepper

Cut the aubergines into 1cm slices, sprinkle with salt and leave to drain for 1 hour. Pat the slices dry with kitchen paper. Coat the bottom of a frying-pan with olive oil and fry the aubergine slices until golden. Add the tomatoes and garlic, season with salt and pepper and leave to simmer gently for 20 minutes, stirring from time to time.

Pound the anchovy fillets in a mortar with 1 tbsp of olive oil. Stir in the flour, then the milk. Add this mixture to the vegetables and continue cooking for 5 minutes. Check the seasoning.

Preheat the grill to medium. Transfer to a *gratin* dish and cover with a layer of breadcrumbs. Sprinkle with oil and brown under the grill.

Erick Vedel, the famous expert on Provençal cookery and its history, kindly showed me his preferred version of presenting aubergines. It is a reminder that he serves the sauce cold. *Estrasses* are in the *Occitan* language bits of cloth, which the cooked aubergines are thought to resemble.

Les Aubergines en Estrasses

Fried aubergines with a tomato sauce

2 medium-sized aubergines (about 900g)
coarse salt, for sprinkling
1 kg ripe tomatoes, peeled and chopped
2 medium-sized onions, chopped
2 cloves garlic, chopped
olive oil
salt and pepper

Trim the ends of the aubergines and cut them lengthwise into 1cm slices.

Lay them out on a plate or board and sprinkle with coarse salt. Leave to disgorge their juices for 20 minutes before turning and salting a little more. Leave a further 15 minutes. Pat the slices dry with a towel or kitchen paper.

Make a tomato sauce by cooking the tomatoes, onions and garlic in olive and for 20 minutes. Taste and season.

Heat a thin layer oil in the bottom of a large frying pan and fry the aubergine slices over medium heat on both sides until they turn dark in colour and are crisp. Serve with the tomato sauce.

Another dish going under the same name dispenses with the frying; you simply put the uncooked aubergine slices into the sauce and simmer gently for half an hour.

A final review of aubergine recipes brings us to a pair of recipes for a *tian*, which is the name they give in the Midi for an earthenware open dish. The name of the receptacle has given its name to many preparations that can be cooked in it. Here is a way of combining aubergines with courgettes and cheese. It can be served hot or cold. The cheese authentically would be mozzarella, but mozzarella is mostly made industrially these days and is no substitute for a real cheese from unpasteurized milk. That is unless you can find real *mozzarella* made from buffalo's milk under *appellation* rules. This is why the unfermented *Tomme d'Aubrac* or *Cantal cheese*, used also in making the famous *aligot*, is a better substitute.

Tian de Légumes Gratiné

Summer vegetables baked with cheese

2 sprigs of rosemary
3 tbsp olive oil
1 aubergine } all washed and cut in thin slices
2 courgettes } all washed and cut in thin slices
4 tomatoes } all washed and cut in thin slices
2 onions, peeled and sliced
300 g *Tomme d'Aubrac* or *Cantal* cheese, cut in slices
salt and pepper

Preheat the oven to 180C/350F/gas mark 4.

Remove the leaves from one of the rosemary sprigs, keeping the other whole for decoration.

Put a little of the oil in the *tian* and add the vegetables in alternate layers. Season each layer and sprinkle with oil. Tomatoes should be the last of the layers.

Sprinkle with the leaves of one sprig of rosemary, then cover the top with the cheese slices. Bake in the oven for 1 hour. Decorate the dish with the remaining rosemary sprig to serve.

Other *tians* contain eggs, which give a more creamy texture to the finished dish. Some combine courgettes with potatoes (another seasonal marriage), or cheese and anchovy fillets. It rather depends on what you have handy. This one is based on courgettes and tomatoes, invariably in full season together.

Tian Aux Courgettes et Aux Tomates

Baked courgettes and tomatoes

750 g courgettes, cut into 1cm cubes
olive oil
½ onion, chopped
375 g tomatoes, skinned, deseeded and chopped
1 large clove garlic, chopped
3 large basil leaves, chopped
4 tbsp parsley leaves, chopped
3 eggs
grated nutmeg
3 tbsp grated Gruyère or Comté cheese
butter, for greasing
salt and pepper

Preheat the oven to 190C/375 F/gas mark 5.

Put the cubed courgettes in a dry frying pan (use one with a lid), salt well and cook uncovered over a low heat until the juices run. Add a little oil, cover with the lid and cook until soft.

Heat more oil in another pan, soften the onion, then and add the tomatoes and garlic. Cook until well reduced, adding the basil, half the parsley and season. Combine this mixture with the courgettes.

In a bowl, beat the eggs well seasoning with salt, pepper and nutmeg, adding the cheese and the remaining chopped parsley. Mix with the vegetables.

Butter your *tian* and pour the vegetable and egg mixture into it. Cook for 20 minutes.

It is virtually impossible to keep up with the development of the courgette from a tiny 15cm dwarf to the giant monster that graces our harvest festivals. The former are delicious, the latter boring, so while the plants are maturing in the *potager*, you have to eat them most days. By the end of August, one wonders whether one wants to see another one– that is, until the baby ones of the succeeding season begin to appear. Apart from the inevitable twinning with tomatoes, there are other delicious ways we have found to cook them in the South-West, such as this simple method, which we found on a torn piece of a local newspaper.

Les Courgettes au Beurre

Fried courgettes

3 medium-sized courgettes
60 g butter
salt and pepper

With a cheese-grater or on a mandoline, grate the courgettes without peeling away the skin (you could use the julienne shredder of a food processor).

When ready to serve, not before, heat the butter to foaming point in a wide *sauté* pan. Add the courgettes unseasoned, tossing them frequently, for half a minute.

Tip into a warm serving dish, then season them and serve.

o

Another vegetable that poses a challenge for the gardener/cook is the *haricot vert* (green bean), so delicious when young and finger-sized, less attractive but still very useful as the season goes by. The plants can go on yielding as long as the warm season lasts, and even into autumn in some years. It must be stressed that *haricots verts* are not in any way like runner beans, although they can be grown on stakes as well as close to the ground as dwarf plants. The daily yield of *haricots* from the garden is a challenge to the ingenuity of the cook, and very many ways have been devised of using them. Simply steamed and served with a *persillade* of parsley and garlic, they make a fine accompaniment to meats. A variation is this version, using onions as a feature.

Les Haricots Verts Aux Oignons

Green beans with onions

2 tbsp sea salt
300 g *haricots verts*, topped and tailed
1½ tbsp butter
2 medium-sized onions, finely chopped
chopped parsley
freshly ground black pepper

Fill a large pan with 4 litres of water and add the salt. Bring to the boil.

Fill a large bowl with ice. Cook the beans in the salted water for 4 minutes (calculated from the time the water comes back to the boil). They should remain slightly crunchy. Drain them and put them into the iced bowl. Drain again and wipe dry.

Melt the butter in a heavy frying pan and soften the onions in it for a few minutes. Add the beans and cook until they are tender but still a little firm. Add the chopped parsley, season and serve immediately.

LES HARICOTS TARBAIS AND OTHER WHITE BEANS

Haricots verts give way at the end of the summer to the white beans that mature in a similar-looking pod. They are a staple winter nourishment as well as a flavour-giving ingredient for *daubes* and other slow-cooked dishes. There are various varieties coming from all over France: the *cocos* from Paimpol in Brittany, which are sold in huge bags of several kilos for drying and conserving over the winter; others from Soissons in the north-east of France– but none compare with the *haricots Tarbais* produced in the lee of the Pyrenees close to Lourdes (though their neighbours in Pamiers might not agree). A more generic style is called *lingots*.

How is it that, although first planted by the local bishop at the beginning of the 18th century and attaining a production of 3,000 tons in 1881, few people in our lifetime had heard of the *haricot Tarbais* except a handful of local market gardeners?

The answer lies in the way it used to be grown– climbing among the local old-fashioned maize plants. Mass cultivation of maize was introduced in the 1950s, and harvesting by machine was incompatible with hand-picking the beans, so production fell in the last quarter of the 20th century to a mere 55 hectares, spread over 650 small growers.

As with other industries threatened with eclipse (e.g. the cheeses of the Cantal and the wines of Marcillac), revival became the inspiration for a handful of enthusiasts.

A cooperative was formed in 1988 and is at the heart of the renaissance, with hundreds of local gardeners cultivating by hand a few individual bean plants.

What is so special about the *haricot Tarbais*? First its size: it doubles in volume with cooking. Second, once boiled, it can be added to other dishes such as cassoulet and *haricot de mouton* without losing its texture. It has an intense and individual flavour, especially when cooked from the pod. *Tarbais* can be bought fresh in retail outlets all over the South-West when in season (late August to mid-September). They should be eaten within a few days, or should be dried. They can also be frozen. Dried, they require overnight soaking and, fresh or dried, an hour's cooking. Do not salt until after cooking; they may otherwise burst, or they may become hard and will require longer cooking.

Tarbais are more expensive than the other white beans mentioned above which are still popular (perhaps for cost reasons). In dried form, *Tarbais* can be bought from good food shops, or online from the cooperative. Here is just one way that haricots *Tarbais* can be put to good use. The recipe is poached from the famous village of Moustiers, near Monaco, but has a South-West feel about it.

Les Haricots Tarbais à la Moustierenco

White beans South-West style

150 g *haricots Tarbais*, soaked overnight if dried
bouquet garni
2 medium-sized onions, one stuck with a clove, 1 chopped
2 sticks celery
olive oil
1 large tomato, peeled and chopped or 1 tbsp tomato concentrate
1 clove garlic, chopped

Place the beans in a large pan of boiling water so that they are covered to three times their depth. Add the *bouquet garni* and the onion stuck with a clove and the celery. Cook for 10 minutes on a high heat, then reduce the heat and continue cooking for a further 40 minutes. Drain, reserving the cooking water (discard the vegetables).

Meanwhile, in another pan, heat the oil and sauté the chopped onion until golden but not brown. Add the tomato and simmer together for 5 minutes. Add the beans, the garlic and enough of the reserved bean water to cover, then put a lid on the pan and simmer for 20 minutes. Check for seasoning. The beans should be tender but not mushy.

Summer vegetables don't have to be presented in a *ratatouille*-kind of way with a lot of oil and liquid. They can be quite simply roasted, with a little planning from the cook, because he or she needs to start the preceding day.

Les Légumes Rôties

Roasted vegetables

1 medium-sized aubergine (about 450 g), roughly chopped
1 bell pepper (any colour), roughly chopped
1 large tomato, quartered
2 small courgettes, roughly chopped
1 onion, roughly chopped
2 garlic cloves, chopped
1 lemon, half of it juiced, the other half grated for its rind
olive oil
salt and pepper
12 stoned black olives, halved or quartered according to size, to serve

Put the vegetables in a roasting tin with the juice of half the lemon, season with salt and pepper, add enough oil to coat, and give the vegetables a stir. Cover and leave overnight.

The next day, heat oven to 200C/400F/gas mark 6. Roast the vegetables, uncovered, for 1 hour. Sprinkle the finished dish with the grated lemon rind and chopped olives. Add more oil if you like. This dish can be served lukewarm.

There can be few more popular fruits than the tomato (which is not classified technically as a vegetable). They are on sale everywhere the whole year round, coming from all over the world and all sorts of artificial environments. In the south of France, real, garden-grown tomatoes are not available until the middle of July. Anything you may find before then may look like a tomato, but is full of core, little flesh, and no flavour.

Varieties come and go according to fashion. Recently the picturesquely named *coeur de boeuf* has been adopted by producers who think that any tomato with wrinkles is entitled to the name. A real *coeur de boeuf* is without wrinkles and is indeed the shape of a heart. It has few pips and not a great deal of juice, which is an advantage seeing that so many recipes call for the rejection of both. Instead it is full of fruity flesh, and, when fully ripe, is incomparable. Other notable varieties are St Pierre and the early-maturing Marmande, called after the town of that name in Lot-et-Garonne where the variety was created and first commercialized. Down there they have a way of preparing them to accompany in particular a *magret de canard*.

Les Tomates Confites de Marmande

Baked tomatoes

Marmande tomatoes
olive oil
sugar

Preheat the oven to 150C/300F/gas mark 2.

Cut the tomatoes into halves or quarters according to size. Put them into an oiled oven-proof dish, sprinkle them well with sugar and bake in the oven for 1 hour until *confites*.

Stuffed tomatoes are widely served in restaurants but are seldom worth a second thought. They need careful preparation and anything but fresh breadcrumbs will not do at all.

Les Tomates Farçies

Stuffed tomatoes

4 large tomatoes (Marmande or *coeur de boeuf* for preference)
garlic, to taste (2-4 cloves)
fresh breadcrumbs
leaves of parsley, basil and thyme, all finely chopped
best olive oil
salt and pepper

Preheat the oven to 190C/375F/gas mark 5.

Slice the top off each tomato and discard them. Squeeze out the seeds and liquid from the tomatoes into a bowl (discard). Make a mixture of the garlic, breadcrumbs and herb, season, and moisten with plenty of olive oil.

Cover the base of an oven-proof dish with oil, put in the tomatoes and fill them with the stuffing mixture. Pour over more oil to moisten them and bake for 30 minutes.

o

More often than not, the tomato is served in salads, sometimes mixed with other summer vegetables.

La Salade de Tomates et Courgettes

Tomato and courgette salad

3 medium-sized courgettes, sliced
a few spring onions or 1 large shallot, sliced thinly
2-3 medium-sized tomatoes, chopped

For the vinaigrette
vinegar
salt and pepper
dash of ground cumin
pinch of piment d'Espelette
olive oil

Slice the courgettes and spring onions (or shallot) and steam them for 5 minutes.

Mix together the ingredients for the *vinaigrette* and use to dress the courgettes while they are still hot, adding the tomatoes. Toss well and leave to drain.

Dress with a little more olive oil. If you like you can add some steamed fennel or *haricots verts*.

o

At the end of the season most people will be left with a lot of unripe tomatoes. A dear friend and neighbour suggests this way of dealing with them.

La Salade de Tomates Vertes

Salad of unripe tomatoes

2 large unripe tomatoes
1 tbsp salt
1 tbsp red wine vinegar
olive oil
chopped herbs (as available)

Cut the tomatoes into four or six wedges and put them in a plastic bag with the salt and vinegar. Shake them gently around in the bag and leave to rest for at least half an hour.

Pour off all the liquor, then dress the tomatoes with oil and chopped herbs.

The globe artichoke is a plant that requires good soil, plenty of moisture and freedom from frost in the winter. Sadly, we cannot provide or guarantee any of these in our farmhouse *potager*, which no doubt explains why one of our first and best friends in the region said we should never try to grow them. We have tried and he was right.

The French cultivation of the artichoke is nowhere near as extensive as in neighbouring countries, the plant being particularly suitable to the Mediterranean climate. Nevertheless, it is popular, not so much in rural communities as in the towns, and lends itself to many interpretations. One of the best known of these is the Provençale speciality calling for young specimens. 'Barigoule' is said to be a corruption of the old word 'farigoule' meaning thyme.

Les Artichauds à la Barigoule

Artichokes cooked with thyme

4-8 young artichokes according to size
olive oil
1 medium-sized onion, chopped
1 slice salt belly of pork, cut into strips (optional)
120 ml dry white wine
1 sprig of thyme
pepper

Prepare the artichokes by cutting off any sharp leaf points and pulling off any coarse lower leaves. Break off the stalks. Larger artichokes should be cut into 4 and their chokes cut out.

Cover the base of a thick-bottomed lidded casserole with oil. Over a medium heat, add the onion, pork and artichokes (with their stalks), cover and cook to brown the contents lightly, then add the wine, thyme, season with pepper and add 120ml water. Reduce the heat and cook for up to 1 hour, stirring the contents from time to time and adding more water if necessary.

Fresh chestnuts are best roasted round the fire if you have the patience and the special pan with holes in the bottom. However, nowadays you do not have to wait for the season to enjoy them because they are so readily available, frozen or vacuum-packed. Try this garnish, which is very good with roast game or pork.

Le Confit de Petits Oignons Aux Châtaignes et Aux Noix

Dish of small onions, chestnuts and walnuts

2 tbsp duck or goose fat
12-20 small onions according to size, allowing 3-5 per person
16 walnuts, cracked and shelled
120 ml dry white wine
4 tbsp chicken stock
24 chestnuts, peeled
salt and pepper

Melt the fat in a heavy frying pan, add the onions and cook gently for about 10 minutes until softened but not brown.

Keeping the walnut kernels in quarters, if possible, add them to the onions, season, add the wine and stock and simmer gently, uncovered, for 40 minutes.

When the onions are cooked, the liquid should have reduced by about one third and be slightly syrupy. Add the chestnuts and let them absorb some of the juices for a further 10 minutes over a low heat. Check for seasoning.

Another useful garnish, this time for beef or veal perhaps, can be made from mushrooms and celery.

Les Champignons à L'Étuvée

Stewed mushrooms

12 chestnut mushrooms about 5cm in diameter (more if smaller)
1½ tbsp duck or goose fat
2 sticks celery, sliced
100 ml white wine (not too dry)
salt and pepper

Remove the stalks from the mushrooms and slice them into fine rings, keeping the mushroom heads themselves whole.

Choose a pan with a tight-fitting lid which will take the mushrooom caps in one layer. In this melt the fat then add the celery and the mushroom stalks and cook them without browning. When this mixture has softened, lay the mushroom caps whole on top of it. Add the wine and bubble for a few minutes. Add seasoning and cover. Allow to simmer gently for 25 minutes. The mushrooms should be tender but not soggy.

Cauliflower does not often appear on tables in the South-West, but the Basque country provides a very tasty way of serving it. Naturally the local *piment* plays a prominent part. It is useful for the cook to know in advance whether those who are going to enjoy it like their *piment* strong or less so.

Le Chou-Fleur au Piment

Spicy cauliflower

3 tbsp extra virgin olive oil or walnut oil
1 piment d'Espelette or 2 tsp ground piment
1 large clove garlic, finely chopped
1 cauliflower, divided into florets
salt

Sever the florets from the cauliflower stem, keeping them whole. A bread knife is good for doing this.

Cover the base of a sauté pan with the oil and allow the pepper and garlic to sweat in it over a gentle heat for 15 minutes or so. This will extract some of the flavour from the pepper while at the same time turning the oil a pretty orange colour.

Meanwhile, steam the cauliflower florets for 6 minutes, and drain them. Add the pieces to the pan, which should then be placed on a metal protector over the lowest possible heat and left for at least 45 minutes. Do not allow it to boil. Turn the florets over in the pan juices from time to time, so that they become evenly coloured and flavoured with the garlic and pepper. Do not allow them to become soggy or overcooked. They should have plenty of texture when served with the pan juices and contents poured over them.

LES DESSERTS

WHEN WE FIRST CAME TO the South-West, the menu in the simpler restaurants offered you both cheese and fresh fruit ('f and f' as we used to say) and no confected desserts. Today it is all change. Cheese is sometimes offered at a supplement to the *prix fixe* either as a separate course or as a dessert. Gone is the bowl of fresh fruit, except that a fruit salad (*compôte de fruits*) makes an occasional appearance. Instead, the fashionable choice rests between something chocolatey or a sugary confection topped with a mountain of *crème chantilly*. Or both.

Not being admirers of *crème chantilly*, we have set out to discover desserts more in the traditional line, because today they are obligatory to satisfy the contemporary sweeter taste. A meal without one is regarded as incomplete.

Fruit tarts are one way round this problem, and can be either made at home or bought at the nearest *boulangerie*. Avoiding for the moment the inevitable chocolate, here is a simple summer fruit tart.

La Tarte Aux Fruits

Fruit tart

For the pastry (*pâte sablée)*

125 g butter, softened
50 g icing sugar
1 egg yolk
30 ml water250 g flour

pinch of salt

For the filling

80 g unsalted butter, plus extra to grease
70 g caster sugar
70 g ground almonds
3 eggs, beaten
20 ml rum or other spirit
red fruits according to season: raspberries, red or black currants, strawberries, *fraises des bois*
2 tbsp redcurrant jelly

Preheat the oven to 200C/400 F/gas mark 6.

To make the *pâte sablée,* cream together the butter and sugar until smooth and light in colour. Gradually add the egg yolk and then the water, mixing in a little at a time, and finally add the flour and combine into a smooth dough. Wrap in cling film and chill for an hour or so until firm.

Butter a 22-23cm tart tin, roll out the chilled pastry and use it to line the tin, then prick the base all over. For the filling, mix together the butter and sugar then add the almonds. Incorporate the beaten eggs and the spirit.

Fill the tin with this mixture and bake it for 20 minutes. Chill.

Fill the tart with the fruits and glaze with redcurrant jelly melted with 1 tbsp of water.

Apricots are one of the few fruits that are more interesting cooked than raw, when they seem turnipy and rather juiceless, although those coming from Roussillon are justly admired. In season from June to August, they make a delicious summer tart. Once again, *pâte sablée* is used, as detailed in the preceding recipe .

La Tarte Aux Abricots et Aux Amandes

Apricot and almond tart

Serves 6

800 g apricots
100 g ground almonds
100 g butter, melted
100 g vanilla sugar, plus extra to sprinkle
3 eggs or 2 eggs and 1 egg white, beaten
2 tbsp rum or other spirit
300 g *pâte sablée* (as above)
toasted flaked almonds, to serve

Preheat the oven to 200C/400F/gas mark 6.

Wash the apricots, cut them in half and remove the kernels.

Make an almond cream by mixing together the ground almonds, butter and sugar. Blend in the beaten eggs and alcohol.

Line a flan tin (or six individual tartlet tins) with the pastry, and, if there is any left over, twist it to make two 'ropes' and put them round the rim with some egg white. Prick the base all over with a fork.

Pour the almond cream into the flan case and arrange the half apricots cut-side down in it. Any remaining can be sliced and fitted in between. Bake for 20 minutes or until nicely browned. Sprinkle with sugar and/or toasted flaked almonds.

Apricots can be enjoyed in many ways. Our local friends make good supplies of jam to see them throughout the winter. They can be bottled or dried to use later in cooking. Here is a way of enjoying apricots without making a tart.

Les Abricots Poêlés Aux Épices et Aux Amandes

Cooked apricots with spices and almonds

8 apricots
50 g sugar
20 g butter
70 g almonds, chopped
vanilla pod, whole
2 tbsp raisins
spices to taste (*e.g.* cinnamon, nutmeg, allspice or cardamom)
4 mint leaves, chopped

Halve the apricots and remove and discard the kernels. In a wide frying pan, make a caramel with the butter and sugar.

Add the apricots, nuts, raisins, vanilla pod and spices. Add a little water and cook for 5 minutes on a hot flame.

Serve *tiède,* garnished with chopped mint.

o

Apple trees are to be found everywhere, even on roadsides where passers-by are free to pick them if they can be bothered. Most of them are old varieties, some more tasty than others, sometimes quite sour and better used for making cider. Golden Delicious are of course everywhere, much scorned by *gourmets*, although friends of ours assure us that, if kept longer than usual, they can indeed live up to their name. Apples are a popular base for tarts, although we have not found them much used in the cooking of main dishes. The following recipe shows how they can be used as a concentrated relish on their own, or as an accompaniment to cold meats such as pork or duck.

Les Pommes Aux Epices

Spiced apples

4 dessert apples (any kind)
¼ tsp ground cinnamon
¼ tsp ground nutmeg
6 cloves
60 g brown sugar
1 orange, juiced, plus a piece of the peel
2 tbsp dried fruit (currants and raisins)
30 g unsalted butter
2 tbsp Calvados or other spirit

Preheat the oven to 160C/140F/gas mark 3.

Peel and core the apples and cut them into half inch pieces. Put into an ovenproof pan with a close-fitting lid and add all the other ingredients. Heat the pan gently on the hob to melt the butter before transferring all to the oven.

Cook uncovered for at least 3 hours until the fruit is soft. The longer you cook it the darker it gets. Leave to cool a little before putting it into sterilised jam jars with screw-top lids.

This makes enough to fill 2 x 1 lb jam jars. It will be good for months.

Peaches are one of the principal delights of summer in the South-West, grown everywhere from the Pyrenees to the wilder country of the Aveyron. Apart from the usual varieties of white or yellow there are also the wild *pêches de vignes*, so called because they used to grow in between the rows of grapevines. They are usually much smaller, and, though not as sweet, are deliciously refreshing. Nowadays very popular and cheap are the flat peaches, commercially bred from the *pêches de vignes*. The following recipe is one way of enjoying them, although it can be applied to all kinds of peach.

Les Pêches Plates Flambées

Flat peaches cooked in Grand Marnier

6 flat peaches
25 g butter
50 g caster sugar
50 ml Grand Marnier
1 tsp piment d'Espelette

Cut the peaches in half and remove the stones.

To make the caramel, set a frying pan over a moderate heat, and add the sugar and butter. Cook for around, stirring as the sugar melts and dissolves and starts to colour. Do not allow it to colour too much.

As soon as the caramel has acquired a golden brown colour, add the peaches to the pan and cook over a low heat for 5 minutes. Add the Grand Marnier, bring to the boil and carefully set alight, allow to reduce for about five minutes, then leave to cool.

Peel the peaches and divide them among 6 small plates. Dress them with the juices and sprinkle with the pepper. Serve lukewarm.

When the peach season has finished and autumn beckons, thoughts can turn to quinces, invaluable fruit for their long-lasting qualities and for the aromas they give the kitchen as they mature. From the tree they are hard to peel and seem as if they might need hours of cooking, but that is not the case. Here is an easy alternative to the more usual way of serving them in a sweet wine syrup.

Les Coings au Four

Baked quinces

4-5 small or 2 large quinces
300 g sugar
100 ml water
200 ml fresh lemon juice, plus the zest of 2 lemons
3-4 bay leaves
1 vanilla bean

Preheat the oven to 180C/350F/gas mark 4.

Peel and core the quinces and cut them into wedges by cutting them in half from top to tail and then cutting each half into 3 wedges.

Spread the wedges out in one layer in a large, heavy-bottomed gratin dish or roasting tin. Sprinkle with the sugar and cover with the water and lemon juice. Add the zest, bay leaves and vanilla bean.

Cover tightly with foil and roast for 30-35 minutes until tender. Will keep in an airtight container in the fridge for several weeks.

The cacao tree was first planted by the native tribes of Central America. It was introduced to the West Indies by the conquering Spanish. The method of producing chocolate from the beans was jealously guarded for many years, reaching Europe only in the 17th century when it became as popular and fashionable as a beverage as coffee or tea. The fashion died but was revived in the 19th century when it reappeared in solid form.

In Spain, chocolate soon developed as a thriving industry in the Basque country, soon crossing the mountains to France where Bayonne became and remains an important manufacturing base.

The current fashion for dessert based on chocolate has, not surprisingly, developed a Basque twist.

La Mousse au Chocolat Basque

Chocolate mousse Basque style

125 g dark chocolate, chopped
75g unsalted butter
3 eggs, separated
½ tsp piment d'Espelette
50 g caster sugar

In a bain-marie or over a bowl of hot water, melt the chocolate. Add the butter, mixing well to get a homogeneous paste. Add the egg yolks and the *piment* and stir to combine. In a separate clean bowl, whisk the egg whites with the sugar , then gently fold into the chocolate mixture.

Divide the mousse into 4 ramekins and refrigerate them for a few hours or even overnight.

Many of the recipes in this book call for cheese of one kind or another, either in the cooking, or eaten quite simply, raw, at the end of a meal. But it is as well to remember that the South-West is home to some of the finest cheeses in the world, ranging from the Cantal/Salers/Laguiole varieties made from cows' milk to the ever-popular Roquefort and the hard Pyrenees varieties made from ewes' milk, not forgetting the countless kinds of goat cheeses, some made industrially and others direct from the homestead or the local farm.

Most cheese is pressed at some stage during its making, to rid it of surplus liquid. But specialist cheese shops and local farms who supply from the door can provide fresh cheese in its basic and unpressed version– natural, unsalted and therefore of twin use either on its own or as a part of a dessert.

Le Fromage Fermier Aux Amandes

Fresh cheese with almonds

350 g fresh unpressed cows' or goats' cheese
salt and pepper
60 g slivered almonds, lightly toasted
hazelnut or walnut oil

Drain the cheese well and put it into small moulds or ramekins to chill. Turn them out when compact on to small plates, season with salt and pepper and spike the top surfaces with the almonds. Drizzle the oil over and serve.

Iced sweets are all the rage, especially in summer. Commercial ice cream is readily available and of a very high standard, so it is hardly worth going to the trouble of making your own at home. Many people will look no further than serving it as an accompaniment to simply cooked fruits, but we have memories of an ice cream given to us at an hotel in Gascony. We did not ask for the recipe, but we devised our own interpretation.

Le Glace Caramel au Beurre Salé

Caramel ice cream

For the caramel
4 heaped tbsp sugar
2 heaped tbsp butter demi-sel

For the ice cream
3 egg yolks
150 ml single cream or *crème fleurette*
1 heaped tsp coarse sea salt
150 ml double cream

Prepare the caramel by warming the sugar in a heavy-based pan until it dissolves and starts to ooze liquid and turns a golden brown colour. Add the butter and stir until you have a perfect blend. Set aside.

To make the ice cream, put the egg yolks into a double boiler over a pan of gently simmering water. Heat the single cream nearly to boiling point and add it with the salt to the yolks. Continue stirring until the mixture thickens. Leave to cool. Whip the double cream lightly and fold it in. Pour into a container for freezing, stirring the caramel gently, leaving streaks of it through the ice cream. Freeze, either in the deep-freeze or in the ice-making compartment of your refrigerator, turned to its coldest setting.

Ices do not, of course, have to contain cream at all. Restaurants will often offer you a variety of fruit flavours, either in the form of ice cream or as sorbets. But not many will propose this unusual *sorbet de luxe.* Elsewhere made with Chablis and best Cognac brandy, it is hardly less good when made with a good local dry white wine and some basic Armagnac.

Le Sorbet Sud-Ouest

Sorbet à la South-West

Serves 6

250 g sugar
150 ml water
½ bottle Gaillac or other dry white wine
100 ml Armagnac
juice of 1 or 2 lemons according to size

Make a sugar syrup by dissolving the sugar in the water and bringing it slowly to the boil. Leave to cool.

When the syrup is cold, stir in the wine and the Armagnac. Add some strained lemon juice, tasting as you go for balance.

Turn the mixture into a bowl and freeze. When it starts to solidify around the edges (after 1 hour or so in the freezer), turn the edges into the middle and continue stirring often as it sets in order to form a smooth consistency– the more stirring the better. The sorbet should never become really hard, but should have the consistency of fine snow. Serve in chilled glasses to prevent its melting too quickly.

The recipe for another sorbet was given us by the famous chef, Michel Guérard, who at the time was not only running his famous *cuisine minceur* establishments at Eugénie-les-Bains, but also a relatively more modest enterprise at Barbotan in the Armagnac district. His wine-based sorbet uses a red wine from Madiran instead of the white, and manages to dispense with the Armagnac.

Le Granité au vin de Madiran

Sorbet of Madiran wine

150 g sugar
100 ml water
½ bottle of Madiran wine
juice of half a lemon
juice of half an orange

Make a sugar syrup by dissolving the sugar in the water and bringing it slowly to the boil. Allow it to simmer for 5 minutes, then leave to cool.

Add the wine and the strained fruit juices, stir well and freeze. As in the above recipe, stir the sides of the *granité* to the middle. Continue to stir until you have a fine mush of frozen granules. This may take longer than you think because the alcohol in the red wine freezes at a lower temperature than other liquids.

Most French bakers are also *pâtissiers*, in that they sell tarts and cakes. These are always beautiful to look at, examples of architectural excellence, crafted and decorated with extreme care and precision. They form the epilogue to birthday celebrations and other special occasions which call for some personal tribute, often when there has already been one dessert.

More simply prepared cakes can also be made at home, and this one features yoghurt, which has become a staple dairy food during the past 30 years.

Gateau au Citron et Yaourt

Lemon yogurt cake

This cake is more attractive if baked and served in a medium sized Bundt tin, which is ring-shaped and has a deep hole in the middle. But you can also use a standard shallow 23cm cake tin, which will yield an equally delicious if not so spectacular a result.

125 g butter
400 g sugar
2 eggs
350 g flour
½ tsp baking soda
salt
250 g plain full fat yoghurt
zest from 1 lemon

Preheat the oven to 180C/350F/gas mark 4.

Butter the cake tin. Put the butter and sugar into a bowl. Beat in the eggs, one at a time. When well mixed, add the flour and then the baking soda, salt and yoghurt. Finally, add the lemon zest.

Transfer to the cake tin and bake for 50 minutes or more if necessary, testing with a skewer from time to time until it comes away clean and the cake has obtained a good golden colour.

LES BOISSONS

THE WINES OF THE SOUTH-WEST need no commendation from a cookery writer. They have become internationally known and admired over a long period of improvement and commercial promotion. Suffice it to say that the region can produce wine of every style, from dry, sweet, white, red, sparkling or fortified to brandy. Perhaps the South-West is the only region that can provide wine for all kinds of food. Dry whites from Gaillac, both still and sparkling; light reds from Marcillac; bigger ones from Cahors and Madiran; and not forgetting the luscious sweet wines from Monbazillac and Jurançon. The fruits of the region can be distilled into *eau-de-vie*: in turn, the *eau-de-vie* can be used to fortify unfermented grape juice. Locally you can still find specialities that do not seem to export themselves to other parts of the region but that provide a useful variation to the usual repertoire of *apéritif* drinks. It is good sometimes to get away from the kirs, the martinis and the pastis.

During the last century, everyone drank wine with their meals, usually diluted with water. It was usually fairly awful stuff, but free because it was usually made from home-grown vines. So now that the regional wines made away from home have gradually increased in quality and price, wine is no longer always consumed at table. Water and beer seem to be acceptable substitutes. The bourgeoisie in particular have nonetheless retained their preference for and even love of wine. Those who make wine for a living, as opposed to those who have a few rows of wine for their own private harvest, are having to look further afield, internationally even, for markets.

At the end of the meal, some winemakers have their own 'dessert wine', *vin cuit*, which is said to go well with chocolate and red fruits or alternatively with *foie gras*. It can also be used to *déglacer* a cooking pan– a versatile glass indeed. However, since it originated as a family treat, commercial versions often have little resemblance to the true original, which is nevertheless well worth recording as below. It contains nothing but pure grape juice and perhaps a few quinces.

LE VIN CUIT

Grape juice is drawn off the grower's vats before it starts to ferment. It is heated in the open air in a cauldron over a wood fire and skimmed regularly. Quinces may be added if wished. Glowing embers are added to the cauldron to give a smoky character. The liquid is simmered to cool overnight.

Next day the juice is filtered off into a barrel, which is stored in the cellars where the rest of the grower's wines are fermenting. Must (grape juice which still contains fruit and pips) is added, so that the cooked juices are activated by the yeasts from the must. The *vin cuit* is racked (i.e. transferred off the lees, to a fresh container) several times over a period of a month, by which time the fermentation has finished. It is then left on its lees for two or three months before bottling.

Some drinks contain no alcohol at all. For example, in the regions where lime trees are grown for their perfumed flowers, there is this popular favourite made from the local produce.

Le Castillou

1 litre water
25 g *tilleul* (dried lime flower leaves and bracts)
40 ml blackcurrant syrup
40 g caster sugar
juice of 2 lemons

Bring the water to the boil, add the *tilleul* and leave to infuse for 5 minutes. Strain and allow the liquid to cool. Add the remaining ingredients, mix well and leave to rest. Drink well chilled.

o

It has become fashionable for some hotels and restaurants to offer cocktails of their own invention, sometimes at rather inflated prices. They make a change and can add spice and novelty to a social occasion. This comes from a nearby village. It features the local *ratafia*, made from Marcillac grape juice fortified with a little *eau de vie*. It is, however, well-diluted as you will see.

Cocktail Belle Rive

Equal quantities:
ratafia
fizzy lemonade
good orange juice (freshly squeezed, for preference)

Mix well and serve with a slice of orange and perhaps a sprig of mint.

o

The strong red wine from Cahors features in a local *apéritif,* which we have not seen outside the region except in Toulouse (where you can find anything). One glass is generally enough, two glasses for the bold. The drink is named after the historically famous archbishop who studied theology at the university of Cahors in 1677 before taking up a bishopric at Sarlat. It is popular for the way it balances the slight bitterness of the walnut with the sweetness of the blackcurrant.

L'Apéritif Fénelon

2 parts Cahors wine
2 parts eau de noix or vin de noix
1 part crème de cassis

Apéritifs are generally served with pieces of finger food of various kinds: small leaves of pink chicory filled with *pâté,* tiny broad beans dipped in sea salt, *grattons* of pork or duck or radishes sometimes stuffed with butter, pieces of smoked *magret* or any *charcuterie* served on toasted *croutons*. We have been served and ourselves serve all these, but perhaps our favourite which never fails to extract murmurs of admiration is this.

Les Biscuits au Parmesan

Parmesan biscuits

Makes 35-50 biscuits

85 g plain flour, plus extra to dust
75 g grated Parmesan cheese
75 g unsalted butter, chilled and diced
pinch of cayenne pepper
⅓ tsp fine salt
¼ tsp ground black pepper
1 tbsp cold water
1 tbsp sesame seeds
1 tbsp nigella seeds
1 egg, lightly beaten

Put the flour, Parmesan and butter in a blender with the pepper and salt. Whizz until you have the texture of fine crumbs, then slowly add just enough cold water to form a ball of dough.

Scrape out on to a lightly floured surface and divide into two equal cylinders 3-4cm in diameter. Wrap in cling film and chill for 4 hours or overnight.

Preheat the oven to 180C/350F/gas mark 4.

Put the sesame and nigella seeds on a piece of cling film and mix them together. Brush the sides of the cylinders with the beaten egg and roll them in the mixed seeds to coat them all over. Wrap again in cling film and chill for 1 hour or so.

Cut the cylinders carefully into thin rounds of 5 mm thickness and lay them out, not too closely, on non-stick baking trays (you can do one or more batches at a time).

Bake for 20 minutes until golden brown.

INDEX

INGREDIENTS

PEOPLE

PLACES

PUBLISHER'S NOTE

CKBK WOULD LIKE TO THANK Tim Hunt and Alison Stattersfield for first introducing us to Jeanne Strang's work. Alison's blog (My Year of French Cookery) and Instagram feed (@recipesswfrance), where she documents her experience in cooking Jeanne's recipes, provided the recipe photography which now illustrates ckbk's digital edition of this book, and of its predecessor, *Goose Fat & Garlic*.

We thank Paul Strang for alerting us to the existence of Jeanne's unpublished manuscript for *Magrets & Mushrooms*, and for his advice and guidance in preparing the book for publication. We also thankful to Orlando Murrin who not only provided the Foreword, but helped extensively with reviewing the manuscript, and to Susan Low for her invaluable contribution as an editor.

ABOUT CKBK

ckbk is a digital subscription service for food lovers, often compared to Spotify for Cookbooks. The ckbk website and app provides unlimited access to the full content of hundreds of the world's most influential cookbooks. The collection includes newly published bestsellers, critically acclaimed award winners and timeless classics as well as historical cookbooks from every era.

To try ckbk for yourself, take out a 14-day free trial of ckbk Premium Membership at https://app.ckbk.com

ckbk

Printed in Great Britain
by Amazon

41381123R00096